The
Things
That
Divide Us

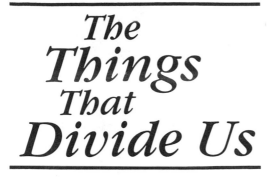

The
Things
That
Divide Us

Edited by
Faith Conlon, Rachel da Silva
and Barbara Wilson

The Seal Press Seattle

Publication of *The Things That Divide Us* is made possible in part by a grant from the National Endowment for the Arts.

Sabon type set by Accent & Alphabet, Seattle.
Printed by Edwards Brothers, Ann Arbor.
Text and cover design by Faith Conlon, Rachel da Silva and Barbara Wilson.
Cover photograph by Deborah Gould Hall, copyright © 1977.

We gratefully acknowledge the following for permission to reprint previously published works:

Robin Becker: "In the Badlands" first appeared in *Plainswoman*. Copyright © 1983 by Robin Becker, reprinted with permission.
Linda Hogan: "Friends and Fortunes" first appeared in *Stand*. Copyright © 1983 by Linda Hogan, reprinted with permission.
Ruth Geller: "Chuck" first appeared in the collection *Pictures from the Past,* published by Imp Press. Copyright © 1980 by Ruth Geller, reprinted with permission.
Valerie Miner: "One of Them" is excerpted from the novel *Movement*, published by The Crossing Press. Copyright © 1982 by Valerie Miner, reprinted with permission of the publisher.
Janice Mirikitani: "Survivor" first appeared in *Amerasia Journal*. Copyright © 1980 by Janice Mirikitani, reprinted with permission.
Pamela Painter: "Sylvia" first appeared in *Ascent*. Copyright © 1976 by Pamela Painter, reprinted with permission.
Evelyn Shefner: "A Hardened Case" first appeared in *The Southern Review*. Copyright © 1979 by Evelyn Shefner, reprinted with permission.
Elaine Starkman: "The Year of Hannah Koznoff" first appeared in *Studies in American Jewish Literature*. Copyright © 1979 by Elaine Starkman, reprinted with permission.

Library of Congress Cataloging in Publication Data

Main entry under title:

The Things that divide us.

    1. Short stories, American — Women authors.
2. Women — Fiction.   3. Interpersonal relations — Fiction.
4. American fiction — 20th century.   I. Conlon, Faith,
1955–   .   II. Da Silva, Rachel, 1951–
III. Wilson, Barbara, 1950–
PS647.W6T48   1985   813'.01'089287   85-8290
ISBN 0-931188-32-6

First edition, June 1985
10   9   8   7   6   5   4   3   2   1

CONTENTS

INTRODUCTION

Diversity, difference, division, divisiveness.

The things that divide us.

This is an anthology of fiction by women that addresses both the positive aspects of diversity among women and the destructive effects of misunderstanding and separation. We chose the genre at the same time we chose the subject it would deal with. That was deliberate. We wanted to discover and publish what women were writing imaginatively about some of the issues that loom so large in the women's movement today.

We didn't really plan on editing this anthology ourselves. Our original idea was to find other women different enough from each other to ensure a range of perspectives. We began spreading the word in hopes of finding two or three women from diverse backgrounds to take on the task of putting the book together. But, like most book projects, what seemed at first a fairly straightforward job proved to be more complex and time-consuming than we or anyone else expected. We soon realized that editing the anthology meant not only selecting the stories, but finding them. It was a lot to ask of our prospective editors, especially since the limited finances of a small feminist press don't tend to include large editorial budgets.

Somewhat reluctantly we considered the possibility of editing the book ourselves. It seemed an imperfect solution, the obvious problem being that our "different backgrounds" didn't amount to much. All three of us are white and, though economic, cultural and geographic factors varied considerably, we all grew up in recognizably middle-class families. One of us is Jewish, another is lesbian and we all have different opinions about what makes for good fiction, but still we felt too "similar." We also felt daunted by the task of outreach. How could we in Seattle manage to contact women in all parts of the country, especially those traditionally under-represented: women of color, poor women, differently-abled women?

In taking the project on, we decided two things. First, to build on the common ground the three of us shared — a commitment to political activism, a strong faith in feminist publishing, and years of working together as editors. Second, to look for a group of women, experienced as editors, writers and teachers, who would help us with outreach and with the editorial process itself — reading and evaluating the stories from varied perspectives. The advisory board eventually came to consist of Beth Brant, Jacqueline De Angelis, Ruth Geller, Kazu Iijima, Aleida Rodríguez, Marj Schneider and Evelyn C. White. They live everywhere in the country except the south, have all been involved in community activism, publishing and/or fiction writing. They are working class and middle class, Black, Mohawk, Japanese-American, Jewish, Cuban, white, visually-impaired, younger, older, lesbian, married, mothers and hold a variety of jobs.

The advisory board was one of the more important aspects of putting the anthology together. By the time we'd found all its members we had already received over a hundred manuscripts from our calls for submissions in women's and literary journals and newspapers. With the efforts of the board, the network extended and more manuscripts came in. It was a year-long process. First we read everything and made preliminary choices, often including stories we had reservations about but that seemed intriguing enough not to pass up. We then sent the stories to the advisory board in three stages over a period of about six months. In the beginning we wondered if the process would be too cumbersome, if we would really be able to stay in touch with advisors scattered all over the country. We needn't have worried — the responses to the stories were prompt, energetic and always illuminating. By the end of the project we felt we had seven new friends whom we seemed to know surprisingly well, though our communication had been almost entirely through the mail.

The project, from the beginning, was sometimes hard to define. One woman writer protested, 'Doesn't *everything* divide us? That's what literature is all about." Another writer offered a very convincing explanation for why we shouldn't limit ourselves to fiction. "Working class women have always written poetry. It's shorter, more accessible. You leave out a whole lot of women when you just include stories."

But we wanted stories, stories about anything as long as it included conflict or the recognition of difference between women. We suggested the issues of racism, anti-Semitism, classism, but hoped for and welcomed others. We were also looking for fresh approaches, convincing dialogue, true-to-life plots and, especially, moving characterization. We wanted to emphasize conflict, after all, and it's hard to have conflict when you don't have at least two people in a story; it's hard to have conflict when the main character is telling the story in the first person or in a barely disguised third person and making all the others into ciphers. This seemed to be where the fictional process diverged most markedly from the auto-biographical impulse to analyze in depth, or the editorial urge to marshal facts in order to convince. The author of a good short story isn't necessarily out to make the reader understand what *she* feels, but to show how two (or more) people can feel two (or more) different things at the same time.

Fiction is both a different form of thinking—thinking in images, in conversations, in fragments heard and remembered, in flashes of insight—and a secondary process in the analytic mode. Stories we read where the author was still sorting out her thoughts and emotions often sounded rough, dogmatic, muddled. Stories where the author caught the tension of an exchange, the pain or sudden clarity of an encounter, the poignancy of a lost moment— even if it weren't totally understood—touched us more subtly, more lastingly.

We tried to choose stories that surprised us, that caught us off-guard, that frightened us at times, that made us angry at other times. The best fiction evokes feelings of all sorts, offers new perspectives, transcends everything we think we know about a subject, and points in directions we've never thought of looking before. Interestingly enough we didn't automatically select the overtly political stories, even though we all consider ourselves political. We read and sympathized, understood many times what the author was trying to express and how hard it was, and then put the story back in the pile in favor of the strong, but often elusive piece that tugged at us emotionally, that made us feel we were in the presence of something living and breathing.

We learned a great deal from who we consciously or unconsciously identified with in the story; sometimes it was alarming how easy it was not to notice the assumptions and prejudices that made one story easy to read, another uncomfortable. Fiction gives voices and faces to conflict. We recognized ourselves and people we know in these stories, but were also encouraged to identify as well with characters unfamiliar to us.

Reading and discussing the advisory board's responses added another dimension to our already lively editorial sessions. We found our choices supported and challenged, the stories praised and criticized. The time and thoughtfulness that went into each advisor's response amazed and sustained us. Each round of manuscript reactions brought new insights, pushing us to reevaluate the stories, to look at each one again with a new awareness. What *was* it we were looking for in a story? Which pieces were really off the mark, inappropriate or possibly offensive in their characterizations? The criticisms from our advisors were refreshingly honest and forthright (as one put it, she "didn't pull any punches in telling [us] which ones should be sent packing"). We found ourselves trying to guess how each would respond, based on previous likes and dislikes, but we were often surprised. Advisors who had agreed that one story was perfect, might disagree vigorously over another, just as we did ourselves.

The questions and issues they raised were challenging. Was it racist for a white author to speak through the character of a woman of color? What really constituted one's class identity—childhood living situation or current circumstances? Were there too many stories from "those of the dominant culture looking into other cultures," as one advisor worried? Could we work with an author, give her what sometimes were clearly political critiques, and hope she could integrate them into her story — or would she respond by suggesting that we were trying to make her story something it just wasn't? These were only a few of the problems we debated endlessly among ourselves and via the mail with our advisors. It wouldn't be fair not to say that a few stories included here were fiercely opposed by one or two advisors and that some stories were dropped with sadness when we were intellectually but perhaps not emotionally convinced by an advisor's criticism.

As we made our final choices, however, we took into consideration the fact that we hope this anthology will be useful as an educational tool for women's studies and other classroom situations. If we learn through experience, then writing that parallels the real experience may be the best way to learn about others. The act of reading a story is, or can be, a process of stepping into a foreign world with both feet, feeling what the characters feel and making their decisions with them. In teaching, getting students to identify with other people or cultures is important. To encourage this process we tried to choose stories that would involve the reader intimately and provoke lively discussion afterwards. Not all the stories use confrontation as part of their resolution but enough do so that comparing the stories or characters from this viewpoint can serve as another avenue for exploring students' gut-level reactions.

There are, of course, gaps in the anthology, serious ones. We received fewer stories from Latinas or Asian women, fewer from differently-abled or older women than we had hoped for. We extended our deadline twice, wrote more letters, made more phone calls, extended our deadline again. More stories arrived, though in smaller numbers than we could have wished. We struggled with the dilemma of whether to postpone the publication of the book indefinitely (and risk losing our NEA funding) while we worked to pull in stories from under- and unrepresented women, or to publish it as it is, a beginning. We chose the latter, knowing that there are many voices still to be heard from, many stories to be told.

The Things That Divide Us is the result of a process that occurred over the course of a year among ten women. We hope it can inspire us to look beyond what we know of one another; we hope it will stir up discussion, urging us to talk, to challenge, to console and to question each other. The things that divide us can define us and help us claim ourselves; they can also be used against us, as ways of keeping us separate from each other and powerless. Only by writing and talking of our differences can we begin to bridge them.

Faith Conlon, Rachel da Silva and Barbara Wilson
May 1985

The
Things
That
Divide Us

IN THE BADLANDS

Robin Becker

WHEN HELEN LEVINE CAME to live with my daughter, I wasn't exactly pleased; in fact, I was against it. They met at the university in Minneapolis where a lot of these odd combinations come about, and they've been here since which is almost two years. Carol got a job teaching math at the Indian school near Turtle Mountain, so they came out here after graduation. I've worked with Indian women from the reservation most of my life at the factory.

Helen grew up in Minneapolis. I don't think South Dakota was what she had in mind; tourist photos of the Badlands, dust storms, endless blank highways. As far as I know, she's the only Jew around except for Ephriam Epstein from Russia who was the first president of the university.

I work for the Bulova Watch Company. During my breaks, I sit with the Chippewa women whose husbands work in the Morell meat-packing plant in Sioux Falls. They see each other on weekends, since the men commute clear across the state. On Monday mornings they gather downtown and climb into pick-ups for the drive. My husband died when Carol was fourteen. He was a quiet man, but when he talked, he had something to say.

They drove down from Brookings on 81 and headed west on 90.

"Mom, this is Carol," she said on the phone. "We blew a tire, but we'll be home tomorrow."

Every sentence had a "we" in it somewhere. We'll be home by such-and-such, or we're looking forward to going house-hunting with you. I'd raised one daughter and I didn't like the idea of getting another. Still, I was luckier than most, whose kids light out for Sioux Falls or Rapid City and never come back except for two days at Christmas.

First thing, Helen wanted to see the Badlands.

"Mrs. Stokes," she said softly, "would you like to come? We'd be happy to have you." She was standing in my kitchen, her dark hair pulled back in a red bandana. She was trying to be kind, but I wouldn't be a party to it.

"No, you girls go. I've been to the National Park more times than I care to remember. I know that place as well as I know anything." I've walked in the gummy Badlands, ruined shoes, stared at fossils while someone read from a guidebook. All alligator bones and sixty-million-year-old imprints. I watched ferrets whipping past, and now they say they're almost gone.

"Extinct is Forever," read her bumper sticker and "Save the Ferret." She was trying to save the world; I just wished she'd forget about my daughter. The postcard she sent me said, "It's so stark — the buttes and knolls. I've never seen such brick-red soil. The mesas have an eerie glow at dusk." She sounded like a brochure from The Chamber of Commerce.

By the middle of August, they'd rented a place that looked like a pioneer shack. That must have been Helen's idea of country life, because Carol knows better. They rented it for the barn, they said.

"If we're gonna live out here, Mom, we might as well have horses," Carol said one Friday evening. She'd started picking me up after work on Fridays. Sometimes I fed her dinner.

"Look," I said, taking some chops from the oven, "if you want to live like cowboys on a cattle ranch, that's your business."

She put her arm around my shoulder. "Oh, Mother, I know it's hard for you." She looked me in the eye. "With Helen and everything, but you could try to get along with her and . . ."

"Aren't I trying? Do I laugh when she asks me what I know about Calamity Jane?" Carol turned her palms up to the sky.

"It's her way of trying to make conversation," she muttered. "You know what I mean."

"Listen, honey, your friend Helen won't be happy until I re-enact the Battle of Little Bighorn here in the kitchen."

"That's not fair," Carol shouted.

"I'll tell you what's fair." I squeezed the kitchen table with both hands. "She wants to see me dressed in a buckskin suit with a prairie rose between my teeth." I strode across the linoleum floor. "Every day it's 'Mrs. Stokes, what do you remember about the thirties?' or 'Mrs. Stokes, were you ever in a duststorm?' or 'Mrs. Stokes, what do you think about the Pathfinder Power Plant?' "

Carol was slumped in a chair. She looked long and lean and athletic.

"What is she, an F.B.I. agent? A sociologist?" I was disgusted. "One question after another. It's not polite."

They got settled in their broken-down farmhouse, and two weeks later, they started looking at horses. They picked me up one Saturday morning in September, and we headed north to Sturgis where I knew an Indian family with horses to sell.

"I'm so glad you could come with us, Mrs. Stokes," Helen said. Carol drove their banged-up blue Toyota, and Helen sat in the back. She kept leaning forward in the space between the bucket seats, making me nervous.

We left the plains for the Black Hills. Occasionally, we saw a gas station or a gift shop. I always found the mountains a relief after that unbroken expanse.

"I'll tell you what kind of horse I'm looking for," Helen began.

I turned to look at her, and our noses almost collided. "Well, first," I said, "I'd better tell you what's available." Carol glanced at me. I knew she was thinking I should take a nicer tone with Helen, but I couldn't. "Appaloosas, pintos, palominos. Don't expect any Eastern horses."

"What kind of horses did you ride, Mrs. Stokes?"

"Anything we could get." Carol glared. "I lived on a farm, you know."

"That must have been something," said Helen emphatically.

"That was something a person was happy to leave! Those winters . . . ah, well, what's the use . . . ." I paused. "Someday Carol, tell Helen some stories."

"Why don't you tell us one now?" Carol asked.

"No," I said.

"Ma, please. Go on."

"For weeks on end, blizzards had us housebound. My father would go out to feed the livestock, but that was all. The farms were far apart, so we hardly saw our friends during the long winters. School was often shut down. When I go visit the Waters on their farm, I wonder how I stood it for so long. We used to cover the windows with burlap bags, on top of every other type of insulation people used back then." I had forgotten about Helen for a second, just remembering and seeing again that farmhouse, those fields, the animals. Coming back gave me a start.

"Carol and Helen?"

"Yes, Mom?"

"Mrs. Stokes?"

"The Pino family are friends of mine; I've known them for years." I wasn't sure how to continue. "I just want you to know that I care what they think of me."

Juana was in the yard when we arrived at their place.

"Hello, Emma!" she called and rushed toward the car. She looked fine—round and tan and healthy.

Juana reached for Carol to give her a hug. "It's been a long time." She wore a flowered-print skirt and a black cotton shirt which pulled at the buttons. I saw the muscles in her arms.

"This is my friend Helen, from Minneapolis," Carol said.

Helen put out her hand and Juana took it in both of hers.

"I'm happy to meet a friend of Carol's," she said.

"Here comes Decklin," I said.

"Well, look who's here," Decklin said softly, putting his hands on my shoulders. I had always loved this boy, my friend's middle son and the sweetest of the three. Now, at twenty-three, he was tall, handsome, strong. His skin was the color of the leaves of the cottonwood tree. This was a joke with us, for as a boy, Decklin was always climbing them.

"Where's Decklin?" someone would ask.

"In a tree," someone else would answer, and we would all laugh. That was when we lived near Edgemont, when Carol's father was mining.

"I hear you want to buy a horse," Decklin said to Carol.

"Well, it's really for Helen. We figured we'd try one and see how it worked out. Then, maybe, we'd try for a second."

"That's how Decklin started," Juana said, "and look what we have now."

Helen asked, "How many horses do you have, Decklin?"

He smiled and said, "Oh, eighteen."

Juana had made a barbecue lunch; we all sat around a table in the yard. Helen wasn't her usual self, which meant she wasn't asking a million questions. I watched Decklin and Carol. Once, a few years back, I'd hoped they might get together. They went out a couple of times, but nothing came of it. Now, they acted like old friends, like children who had grown up together and, as adults, took one another for granted.

"Remember the Crawfords who lived in Custer?" Juana asked reaching for a family-size bottle of Cola. "Well, they moved to Sundance." Juana shook her head. "They'll never find a prettier spot than they one they had here."

"Things change," Decklin said wistfully, looking off to the hills. "They'll be back to visit."

"Once it gets cold, no one's visiting anybody," Juana said. She turned to me. "Emma's one of my closest friends, and how often do we see each other? The cold keeps everyone at home."

"We were just talking about the winter storms Mother remembers. She was telling us about her father's farm."

Right then, something in me wanted to be mean to Helen. I wanted to shock her or shake her or make her see that she was not one of us; she was an outsider, and she would always be.

"Once our dog and her litter of puppies froze in a storm," I said. "They were all dead by the time I found them." I watched Helen's face. Her lips puckered, and when our eyes met, she looked down.

"Iced coffee?" Juana asked.

"There are always accidents on a farm," Decklin said. "Especially in this climate."

I was wondering what Helen was thinking.

"Drink your iced coffee, now," Juana said. "We have to go see the horse Decklin chose for you all."

I was feeling low, like I'd ruined everybody's lunch, especially my own. But I was grateful to see that Juana and Decklin carried on as if nothing had happened. Only Helen was subdued.

Decklin's stables were small and cramped. I'd seen poor farms; I knew the hardship, the sacrifices you had to make to keep a stable of horses, keep them fed, sell them, buy them, breed them.

Decklin unlatched a stall door and put out his hand.

"Hello, Kadoka," he said to the horse. Holding on to his halter, Decklin led him down the corridor towards the door.

Out in the yard, I could see that Kadoka was a beauty. He was big for an Appaloosa, but fine-boned with a handsome head. I was surprised to see that Decklin brought an English saddle from the tack room. Juana and I had always ridden western.

"English saddle for the lady," Decklin said winking at Carol. I wondered for a moment if he knew that they were more than friends.

We all walked over to the ring, a dusty fenced-in area where horses had worn a path in the dirt. Helen took the reins from Decklin. He gave her a leg-up, and, before she had settled into the saddle, Kadoka walked to the gate. I was feeling kind of excited in a nervous sort of way.

"Looks like he knows where he's going," Carol said trying to ease things.

Decklin paused at the gate. Helen bent to adjust the stirrups. For a moment, I felt a thrill, like someone watching a disaster, and I realized that I was hoping Helen would show her true self—make a mistake, make a mess—for everyone to see.

She sat straight in the saddle, hands low, legs motionless. When she trotted close to where I was standing, I could hear her making strange clucking noises; she was talking to the horse.

"He can go English or western," Decklin said leaning on the fence. "Look how smooth he is."

I was ashamed at my desire. I stood there waiting, hoping to see Helen do something foolish or inept.

She began to trot, posting up and down in the saddle. Her knees didn't flap and her body didn't wriggle. She rode like she knew what she was doing.

"He looks like a nice horse to me," Carol said. "What do you think, Mom?"

"Can't tell yet, but he looks all right," I said.

Juana was silent. She stayed out of Decklin's affairs.

I saw Helen lean forward and gather up the reins. The horse, collected, broke into a lope. He had been well trained, I could see.

They went around several times, and then Helen switched directions.

"She's a good rider," Decklin said to Carol. "She has a nice touch."

I could see that Decklin was taken in by Helen, too. Neither Juana nor her son could see that she was unnatural, that she was having a bad influence on Carol.

Helen pulled up in front of us. Sweat trickled down the side of her face.

"I like him," she said to Carol. "Would you ride him and see what you think?"

"Sure."

Helen got off and patted the horse's neck as Carol raised the stirrups. Then, Helen came and stood beside me along the fence. Didn't she know that we were enemies? How could she be so casual?

Carol was a sloppy rider — more confident, more slouchy. She'd ridden English in Minneapolis, but had grown up in western saddles and was used to neck-reining.

"Look!" she called.

She was holding the reins in one hand imitating a cowboy.

Decklin and Juana laughed as she galloped by. Why was I sad? Why did I feel so distant, so separate from my friends and my daughter? Somehow, their pleasure seemed far away, remote as my memories of Carol riding our old buckskin named Buffalo.

Not long after they bought Kadoka, Carol and I started fighting over Helen.

"Take it up with her!" Carol would yell.

"I don't need to take it up with her, because she's not my child, and her life is not my concern," I would reply.

"Then don't come to me with your complaints."

"It was you who brought her here."

Carol's eyes narrowed. "Don't say things like that, Ma." She walked toward me shaking her head. "You don't want to go saying things like that."

"I know what I mean to say, dammit." I'd go off to another

room and feel bad for hurting Carol, but I was the one with the honest hurt.

There were times when I wanted to talk about Carol and Helen with my friends, but I just couldn't bring myself to say the truth. I'd tell myself that no one else could say things I hadn't already thought of. That things were going to be hard for them. But things weren't hard for them. Carol liked her job teaching math. They liked their falling-down farmhouse and their horse and the new friends they made in Rapid City. They weren't lonely for friendship. I kept wondering when Helen was going to get a job. By September, when Carol started teaching, she hadn't found anything. She kept coming up with projects to work on, all for no pay. First, she volunteered at the community center, answering phones, helping with the after-school program. Then she decided to teach a course, Women in Literature, but only four people showed up, including Carol. Next, she decided to write for the local paper; an article called "Rereading Hamlin Garland" and a piece on the girl's track team came out of that.

In November, when Carol couldn't pick me up after work one Friday, Helen came instead. It was desolate and cold. I remember seeing a book called *The Woman Warrior* on the dash.

"Where's Carol?" I said as soon as I got into the car. "Is she all right?"

"She's fine, Mrs. Stokes. She was tired, so I offered to pick you up."

It was snowing by the time we got to my house. "Tell Carol I said she should get some rest this weekend," I said gathering up my things.

"I just want you to know something, Mrs. Stokes. I love Carol very much." She sounded as though she might cry. I heard my voice come out cold and steady.

"I haven't got anything against you personally, Helen. I just wanted something else for my daughter." It was a lie of course, I didn't like Helen and she knew it. She was just trying to anger me with her little confidences.

I stepped out of the car. For a second, I thought we were both thinking the same thing: Carol chose this life; no one forced it upon her. She chose Helen of her own free will.

The following Friday, Helen came again.

"I think it's the flu or something." Helen said. I slammed the door.

"Have you called a doctor?"

"She wouldn't let me."

"Oh, for God's sake."

"I tried, but she said I was an alarmist."

"That girl."

"Mrs. Stokes, where would you like to go?" It was snowing and the wind was blowing. I couldn't tell if Helen was worried about Carol or the weather.

"I'd appreciate it if you could take me home," I said. I huddled in my coat.

"You're welcome to come home with me. I'm sure Carol wouldn't mind." Cars moved slowly down the street. I knew Helen had to get going if she wanted to make it home before the roads froze.

"Looks like we're in for a big one," I said. "I'd better go home."

Helen bit her lip. "Do you mind," she asked, "if we stop at the market on the way?" She turned the key in the ignition. "I think I'd better stock up on a few things, especially if Carol's sick."

"Go ahead. I'll pick up some things, too."

The market was crowded with people. Their boots made the floor slick; twice I had to reach for the cart to keep from falling. Helen knew her mind and steered up the aisles, checking items off her list. I carried a basket which quickly filled.

"Just put your things in with ours, Mrs. Stokes, and we'll figure out the money later."

It was almost six by the time we got out of the market.

"Why don't you just come home with me? We can set you up in the spare room," Helen said zipping up her parka.

Snow fell in thick, wet flakes.

"Think I'll take you up on your offer," I said before I had a chance to stop myself.

"Fine!" said Helen, a big smile spreading across her face. "I'll take you back first thing tomorrow morning."

Carol was in bed when we got there. When we took her temperature, we found that she had a fever of 102 degrees.

"What's all the fuss?" she asked. "Can't a person get sick without everyone making a federal case about it?"

There was a pot of chicken stock on the stove. Helen made some toast and took it along with a bowl of soup into the sick room.

"Sit up, honey," I heard her say softly. I stood in the hall.

"Want some hot tea?" I asked poking my head into the room.

"No thanks, Mom. Maybe later."

The house had a nice feeling to it. Helen and Carol had fixed it up with paintings and things from their friends in Minneapolis. There was a wood stove in the center of the big room which made that part of the house cozy. They had throw rugs and rocking chairs and lots of books and magazines. Everything was used, but there was a warmth.

About eight o'clock, Helen came out to where I was sitting with our dinner. We had soup and chicken and green beans and salad sitting right there by the stove. In her room, Carol dozed.

"There are some young girls like you," I began, "in my factory, who have been trying to start a union." Helen looked up. "Everyone was afraid of them at first, but now—there are two of them—the rest of the women have started to like them."

"Are they from around here?"

"Nope. Chicago."

"What are they doing out here?"

"Organizing," I said. Helen raised her eyebrows.

"And what do you think of them, Mrs. Stokes?"

"I'm not sure," I said.

That night I slept in the spare room. When I woke, I found snow falling and drifts three feet high against the house.

"Good morning," Helen called. A door slammed. "Wow! What a storm." I shivered in my borrowed robe and slippers. She stood with a red face, her felt-lined boots covered with snow. She dropped her mittens and blew on her hands.

"How's Carol?" I asked.

"The same," Helen said pulling off her boots.

I walked down the hall and knocked on her door.

"Come in," Carol called.

She looked pale against the white sheets. When I felt her forehead, I thought I could detect a fever.

"How do you feel?"

"OK," she said. "I'm achey."

"Can I get you anything?"

"How about a ginger ale?"

All day, Helen and I took turns checking on Carol. We kept the stoves going, kept a steady pot of soup cooking, exchanged a few sentences when our paths crossed. I picked up a copy of *Main-Traveled Roads* and read a few stories. Helen fed Kadoka and let him out in their tiny ring for a few minutes. Straining to see him from the window, I could hardly make out his shape in the driving snow. It was dark by three-thirty.

"Can I get you some tea?" I asked when she came in.

She lowered her eyes. "Sure. That would be nice."

I brought two cups of tea and two biscuits which I'd found in the breadbox.

"It was like this when I was a child," I said. "Weeks and weeks like this."

"We could get out if we *had* to," Helen said sipping her tea. "If we had to get Carol to a doctor or something, we could drive to town."

"Snowbound," I said, unable to give any shape to my feelings. I wanted to tell her something, but what? Something to show her I thought she was a real trooper, but I said nothing.

That night we watched a movie called "Missing" on the television. Helen said she'd seen it before, but that it was good and I'd like it. The movie was about an American boy who goes to South America and disappears. His father gets involved in the search to discover what has happened to him.

"I guess the movie means something special if you're a parent," Helen said softly. "It's hard to imagine being in the father's position."

"Not so hard," I said. "It was a good movie, Helen. I'm glad you recommended it." How could I tell her that children disappear in many ways?

"Does your mother work?" I asked.

"Yes. At a museum in Minneapolis."

I was carrying our teacups into the kitchen. "Does she know

about you and Carol?" We both stopped, surprised at my question.

"She does know, Mrs. Stokes, and she's trying to accept it." Helen smiled a sad smile. "She has her problems with me."

We turned off the lights in the kitchen. "Let's check on Carol," I said feeling a sudden tenderness for Helen and her mother.

Carol was asleep. We left the door slightly ajar and said goodnight.

By the following morning, the snow had stopped.

"I'm feeling better," Carol announced during breakfast in bed. "I think I'll go shovel snow and take a ride on Kadoka."

Helen and I looked at each other and laughed.

"What have you two been talking about while I've been dead to the world?"

"Oh," I said. "Things."

I helped Helen shovel a path to the car, while Carol got out of bed for the first time in three days. We left her sitting by the stove drinking hot chocolate and reading.

I kissed her on the forehead like I used to do when she was a child.

Although the roads had been plowed, some power lines were down. We passed cars completely buried in drifts, shops with "closed" signs in the windows.

I felt a stab of melancholy when we parted. Something had changed in the last two days. There was nothing to say or, more truthfully, I am a person who does not say such things.

"We'll call you soon," Helen said, and "I'm glad you were with us."

For Christmas, I bought Kadoka a winter blanket and I got the girls a green glass antique lamp. Helen still troubles me at times, but she is someone real to me—though I have no words for what she means.

HER EX-LOVER

Becky Birtha

I CAN SEE WHEN I TURN the corner onto Second Street that Ernestine is waiting for me. I catch a glimpse of her every few feet as I make my way up the crowded block. She's in the blue slacks she pressed last night, her brown arms bare in a light striped summer shirt. The shirt is loose, hanging out over her slacks. She always wears her shirts that way—I think from some self-consciousness about her size. Ernestine is much more solid than me, but she's taller too, and I think she looks fine the size she is.

She's sitting in a patch of sunlight at the top of the five stone steps that lead up to the travel agency and on into our apartment building. In the spotlight of sun her skin is golden brown, and the full circle of her hair is a brilliant bronze flame. I want to surprise her, to come quietly behind, lean against her broad back and stretch my arms around her. I love coming home to Ernestine—to lock our door upstairs and get lost in her hugs and kisses, and then to hear all about her morning.

She hasn't seen me coming because of the dozens of people jamming the sidewalk. In the middle of a weekday, our block is a zoo. Twelve-fifteen, and all the office workers have been let out for their noontime feeding—including us. But that's why we chose to live downtown, imagining what a relief it would be to come home in the middle of a working day and just be ourselves for half an hour. . . .

As I reach our stoop, I see there's another reason Ernestine didn't spot me coming. There's someone with her, sitting beside her on the white stone steps, and the two of them are talking. I'm close enough now to see who it is. Lisa. Her last lover. Her white lover.

Lisa looks up and sees me coming first, and she says, "Hi, Shirley," with a smile that doesn't look for real.

"Hi, Lisa. Ernie."

Ernie flashes me a swift, silent apology, and gets up to give me a brief, respectable kiss.

"Did the mail come yet?"

"I didn't look," Ernie says, and I get to escape for a minute, ducking into the vestibule to check our box. There's only a circular from some sweepstakes, and another with some grinning sap running for city council. By the time I'm back to Ernestine and Lisa on the steps, they aren't talking any more, and when Ernestine begins again, it's to start explaining things to me.

"You know how Lisa's been planning to move out to California?"

Most of the time, I would just as soon not know what Lisa is planning. But Ernestine has been keeping me posted on this for weeks. Lisa quit her job. Lisa gave notice on her apartment. Two Sundays ago, we went to a porch sale Lisa had, where Ernie actually paid her for a radio that used to belong to both of them. Lisa could probably use the money — for her trip.

"Yeah, sure."

"Well, today is the big day. She's taking off this afternoon."

Lisa chimes in with, "Finally! Huh, Shirley?" She's only half teasing. Lisa knows how I feel about her. Her pale grey eyes watch me for a second, from under the fringe of blond hair. Maybe she expects me to protest politely that she shouldn't put it like that. I haven't got a thing to say.

But Lisa's never at a loss for conversation. She goes chattering on, "I can hardly believe I'm really leaving for good."

I can hardly believe it either. For good! My luck usually doesn't run that way.

"Yesterday, I went down and closed out my checking account at Mutual. I've had an account there for almost ten years. It felt so — final. And then this morning, when I was cleaning out the refrigerator and packing the last few things — you know, my toothbrush and towel and stuff—I started feeling like I was watching myself in a movie or something. It didn't seem real."

"It's a big change to make," Ernie says. "Even if you have been planning it for months."

"Seems like years."

It does seem like years. Because ever since Lisa started saying she was leaving town, she's gotten more and more important to Ernestine.

Last Friday morning we were both in the kitchen—me stirring the grits on the stove, and Ernie walking back and forth putting together lunches, even more quiet than she usually is.

"Shirley?"

I looked over, but she wasn't looking at me—paying a lot of attention to tearing off the lengths of wax paper just so. "Yeah?"

"I wanted to tell you that I made some plans for tomorrow night." She looked up, and my surprise must have been right across my face. We always check in with the other first, before we make a commitment for both of us to do anything. "There wasn't something else we were supposed to do, was there?" she asked.

"Nothing special." I waited for her to go on, but Ernestine never says more than she has to. "What kind of plans did you make?"

She rattled the drawer open and started to rummage for a knife. "With Lisa. We're going out to dinner, and then spend one last evening together."

"All three of us?" I never knew which was worse—being with the two of them together, or being alone, and knowing that they were together somewhere anyway, without me.

Now it was Ernie surprised. She stopped right where she was—standing bent over to one side with her arms up to the elbows in the utensil drawer. "I guess I just automatically assumed you wouldn't be interested."

"In other words, I'm not invited." I couldn't keep the meanness out of my voice. "After all, it's only Saturday night."

"Shirley." Her voice only sounded a trifle impatient, but her hands jerked so quickly the drawer banged shut. "Don't you think it might be good for both of us—for all three of us—if Lisa and I just had one good long final talk? Just to clarify things once and for all."

Ernestine had already started to cut up the cucumber, as if whatever I might answer wasn't going to make much difference. Her hands had found their calmness again, and she stood there, solid and impenetrable, slicing off crisp, thin, even circles. Next to her, everything looked small—the tiny knife in her broad, sure fist, the little squares of sandwiches, the narrow space between the table and the counter that she nearly filled. I could feel the rage rising in me. "I don't understand! I just do not understand what it is you all have so much to say about. What do you do—reminisce about the good old days when she used to treat you like a half-wit and you used to let her?"

Half to herself, she said, "Maybe I never should have told you anything about it." And then, laying down the knife and turning to me, "Look. The woman is leaving town next week. It may be years before I see her again. Maybe never. The least I can do is take her out to dinner."

"You're *taking* her to dinner?"

Neither one of us noticed the rank gray clouds of smoke from the grits on the stove. The pot was scorched beyond saving. We didn't make up for two days.

"You know, Shirley, I'm glad you came home." Lisa is after my attention again. "I wasn't sure if I'd see you or not. Ernestine said sometimes you get rush jobs you have to finish and you can't take your lunch break on time. But I wanted to say goodbye to you both."

To us both. I sit against the railing, meeting that unflinching gaze, not knowing what to say. I'm still thinking about that fight, and so many others Ernestine and I have had because of this woman. Who is supposed to be Ernestine's *ex*-lover, but has just never made her graceful exit off this stage. Claiming some crazy notion that she considers "liberated," about how healthy it is for former lovers to remain friends. I'm thinking about how much I have resented her, how many times I've wished she didn't exist, or could somehow just vanish. Why does she want to say goodbye to me when she's never been my friend?

Not that she didn't try. I guess she saw, as soon as Ernie and I took up with each other, that the only way she could keep from losing Ernestine altogether was to try to be friends with me, too. So she started cultivating a whole new set of interests she thought I could relate to.

The first year Ernie and I were together, Lisa showed up at our place on my birthday with a present for me, all wrapped in gold paper and curly ribbons. I didn't know what to say. All I could think was that I was not about to start buying this white girl birthday presents. She was hanging over me with an excited look on her face like she'd just brought me something she knew I'd wanted all my life but could never afford. "Open it, Shirley."

"Yeah, go ahead." Ernestine was trying to make it seem perfectly natural. "Open it."

I opened it. It was a copy of *Their Eyes Were Watching God*.

I've never had much tact in situations like that, and Lisa could pick it up. "Don't you like Zora Neale Hurston?"

I love Zora Neale Hurston. I've read everything she ever wrote —that's in print. I shifted the book from one hand to the other, not knowing what to do with it. "I already have a copy," I said.

Lisa, of course, looked hurt. One of the things she's an expert at.

Ernestine asked her what she thought of Hurston's book. And it turned out that Lisa hadn't read it herself. So I ended up giving it back to her and sending her home to read it. I didn't really expect her to.

But she finished it and went on to Nella Larsen, and then Ann Petry, and after that Alice Walker. She came back wanting to discuss them all with me. And that was only the beginning. She studied up on black history, and started listening to jazz. She went to some CR groups or something they were having for white women on confronting their own racism. She even started taking dancing lessons. Stuff she never did for Ernestine when they were together.

When they *were* together, it was always Lisa's culture that mattered. Lisa was always making Ernie feel like she didn't even *have* any culture—dragging her around to "openings" and French restaurants all the time, and trying to talk her into going back to school. Nothing about Ernestine was good enough then.

Once, when Ernestine and I first started going together, we were getting ready to go to a party, and I asked her what kind of places she and Lisa used to go.

She shrugged her shoulders, turning to the closet to hunt for the scarf she wanted to wear. "We went to museums and stuff a lot. Concerts."

"What kind of concerts?" At that time, Lisa hadn't developed her taste for jazz yet.

Ernie tried a peacock blue scarf several different ways before the mirror. She answered casually, "We went to hear the symphony orchestra a lot. And sometimes at one of the art galleries we'd go hear a woodwind ensemble or a string quartet or something like that."

Even the words sounded phony in Ernestine's mouth. I could picture her, clapping politely after every charming little étude, making small talk during the intermissions, and "mingling" about as naturally as a Saint Bernard in a pen full of Pekingese.

It made me smolder—even the little bit she would tell to answer my questions. Because I knew Lisa never appreciated Ernie, never understood how special she is, or how much Ernie loved her, never realized how much *she* was getting out of being with Ernie, that it wasn't just a one-way street. Not until they split.

Ernestine finally left her, but Lisa never gave Ernie up. . . .

"I heard New Mexico's supposed to be beautiful, too. Shirley's sister was there on vacation last year, and she said she fell in love with it."

Hearing my name brings my mind back to this afternoon. Ernestine, true to her Libra nature, has been filling in the awkward spaces with words, trying to cover up for my own silence.

"Maybe I'll stop there for a couple of days on my way across," Lisa says. But there's only so much two people can say about places neither one of them's ever been. So the conversation fizzles out again.

The three of us are clumped uncomfortably on the steps, and now they're both looking at me. I can see Ernestine trying to assess what I'm thinking, how I'm feeling.

All of a sudden, I stand up. I need to move. "Did you eat yet?" I ask Ernestine.

"Not yet."

"Would you like—"

"Do you want—" We've both turned to Lisa.

"No thanks," she says. "I just got finished with breakfast. I'll stop for something later, on the road."

"Then I'll just go up and get our lunches," I say. "I have to be back at work by one."

When I start up the steps, Ernestine says, "Shirley?"

"Yeah?"

"Lisa brought over some stuff she had left in her kitchen that she thought we might be able to use. It's on the table and on the counter—you'll see."

When I walk in, every square inch of surface space in the kitchen is crammed with jars and boxes, cans and packages. Soy meal. Alfalfa seeds. Brewer's yeast. Seaweed. Stuff we never use.

Castoffs. Lisa trying to shove these castoffs onto us, that have nothing to do with us, no place in our culture. Just the way she tried to shove them down Ernestine's throat all those years. And I think sometimes she views Ernestine as her castoff, like a dress you give to a good friend, expecting you'll be able to borrow it back if you ever want it again. She doesn't seem to remember it was Ernestine who was through with her.

Sometimes, I get furious with Ernestine for letting Lisa treat her the way she did. For not having more pride.

When Ernestine and I first met, Ernie was all I could think about day and night. But we weren't lovers right away. She was still so swamped with guilt over leaving Lisa, she hardly even noticed I was around. I knew she had Lisa on her mind all the time, and I never gave her any peace over it.

"Don't you know," I used to demand, "that no white person can really love you? That they're only in it for what they can get out of it? Out of you?"

More often than not, she wouldn't answer. Just listen in silence while I'd go on and on—an alert, sharp-eared silence that was a lot more unnerving than her disagreeing with me would have been.

"Don't you see," I'd insist, "why you love her, or think you love her? It's power you're in love with. Privilege. You don't want her. You want to *be* her."

Once she cut me short, asking, "Shirley, if I felt like that, would I bother with you?"

But I couldn't let it rest for a long time, even after I knew Ernie was interested in me. Whenever I found out she'd seen Lisa, or talked to her on the phone, I'd feel compelled to try to make her recognize the weakness she had to overcome. "Can't you understand," I challenged, "that as long as you still love her you're hating yourself? That when you finally come to love yourself, black will be the most beautiful to you?"

"Do you really believe that, Shirley?"

"Do I believe it? Of course I believe black is beautiful."

"No. What you said about me."

We were coming from the women's restaurant, at night, and we both stopped walking, faced each other, and I remember she put her hand on my arm. It was one of the first times she ever touched me, and when she looked into my face I felt like she could see through every slogan and scrap of rhetoric I'd ever spouted off.

"Do you really believe I hate myself?"

I finally came to see that there are things about Ernestine that I may never understand, that I'll never change. One of them is the way she can't help giving of herself to any person—woman or man, black or white, gay, straight—who is unhappy or alone. Another is the way she looks hard for what she likes in people, and won't let the things she doesn't like keep her from loving them. That's what she did—with me.

There was never a winner in any of those arguments with Ernie. There still isn't—winner or loser. The one last weekend went on right through Friday, Friday night, and all day Saturday. And then, Saturday night, Ernestine went out with Lisa anyway. She was gone until one in the morning, and I didn't go anywhere. I stayed in the apartment, seething, cleaning out the drawers in my desk and plotting what I was going to say when she came in. But the second I heard her key in the lock, suddenly I didn't want to fight with her any longer. I don't know why.

We stayed up a long time that night, just holding each other, and both of us were crying.

I find our lunches in the refrigerator, behind a huge container of cottage cheese that's taken up residence on the top shelf. Head back downstairs with them. Outside, I park myself on the steps again and hand Ernie her bag. She thanks me but doesn't open it, and I don't really feel hungry either.

I watch Lisa talking, watch the gestures she makes with her hands. Every time I have ever seen her, she's had something in her hands — proofs of her busy responsibilities — books, keys, or the strap of a heavy bag braced against her shoulder. More often than not, it'll be something she wants to give one of us — a magazine with an article in it she wants me to read, or maybe some notepads her aunt gave her that she thought Ernie could use. But now she is empty-handed. Her two hands hover above her lap, fluttering like the matching wings of a butterfly.

"I've never really been anywhere," she's answering. "I've never been further west than Cincinnati. But I've been dreaming about California all my life. I want to see the giant redwoods and the cable cars." She laughs. "I want to see Shirley Temple's handprints in the sidewalk. . . ."

I watch the people passing on the street. Two young black women approach, chic in expensive hairdos and designer clothes, trying to hurry in the precarious shoes that complete the required outfit. I wonder what this hour holds for them — maybe rushing to get a prescription filled or buying a kid some sneakers, maybe cashing a paycheck and still having time to grab a bite at Burger King.

"Anyway, I think change is good for you," Lisa explains. "And I haven't had enough of it. I've been in the same rut too long. . . ."

In a clot, three white businessmen saunter along, identical in gray, three-piece suits, getting some sun on a leisurely stroll to "The Club" where lunch will be charged to expense accounts. Their heads turn in accord when the two women pass them by.

" . . . but I guess the real reason is that I've finally realized I need to . . . cut myself loose."

I turn to watch Lisa again, and find her eyes on me — flickering with an uncertainty that draws me instantly closer than her most reassuring smile.

"I mean," she says, "the past is past." She shrugs her shoulders, opens her hands.

When she stands up, there seems to be somehow less of her than I've seen before. On the sidewalk, at the foot of the stairs, she looks little — frail. I've always seen her dressed well. But today she's wearing pants that are old and faded, and a gray sleeveless shirt hangs loose on her figure. Its edges are frayed. Her pale hair is wispy and hasn't been cut lately; in the bright sunlight, I can see that some of its strands are not, after all, blond but gray.

"Well, I guess this is it," she says.

"Listen, Lisa." My own voice catches me by surprise. "I hope you'll be happy." Suddenly, I do.

She hugs us both quickly. "I won't say goodbye," she says. We watch her down the block, a small gray figure that gets almost immediately absorbed into the crowd.

I can feel Ernestine looking at me, sideways, trying again to gauge my thoughts. She says, "Well, I guess you're glad that's over."

I guess I should be. But there's a sound underneath her voice that makes me turn to her, fills me up with unexpected remorse. I want to take her in my arms, but we're standing out on Second Street in broad daylight with a hundred people passing by. I say what I can. "I know how much you'll miss her."

Together we walk back toward Main Street. Slowly, silently. Not touching, as we'd like to be, but close.

THE YEAR OF
HANNAH KOZNOFF

Elaine Starkman

THE YEAR THAT Hannah Koznoff came to our school changed my life. It was fate that Miss Allworth sat her next to me and moved Tommy Cwick to the last row. Even though Hannah looked strange with her wild black hair and that ugly red-and-yellow flowered skirt, *anyone* was better than Tom.

As she slid into Tom's bolted-down beat-up desk, I faked a smile. Marsha Samuels, who wore a bra and a cashmere sweater (her mom also played Mah-Jongg with my mom), made a face. Tom Cwick let out a low howl and whispered loudly, "Your father's a Commie."

Miss Allworth rapped her pointer on her desk. "Denise Sherman," she echoed out of her sunken powdered face, "You are the new girl's partner this week. Acquaint her with procedure around Woodrow Wilson. Accompany her to the lavatory at recess. No more girls going alone since the *last* incident." Her thin breast heaved under her man's woolen jacket. Everyone knew that Amadeo, the old waffle man, had entered the building and used the girls' first floor toilet.

I gave Hannah her books, showed her the pencil sharpener, coat rack under the blackboard, paper bin, and extra-credit worksheets. All the time she gazed around with a strange smile like she knew something the rest of us didn't. With that hair, thick eyebrows, tiny pushed-in nose, and silver braces under dark pouting lips, she gave me the creeps.

At 10:25 the old wooden clock with Roman numerals shook the halls of Woodrow Wilson. "Wanna go to the bathroom?" I asked.

Her black eyes narrowed. "Baby face."

"But Miss Allworth said—"

"Miss Allworth says 'jump,' you jump. What are you, a Russian peasant—some *muzhik*?"

Miss Allworth buried herself in her closet and sipped a cup of hot lemon water. Hannah started to stencil her initials, Chicago, 53, on her desk top so I went to the bathroom with Marsha Samuels. "Koznoff doesn't look like she'll make the group," Marsha announced, pulling up her bra strap and flicking lint from her baby blue cashmere.

"Yeah, you're probably right," I said wondering what *muzhik* meant.

When I got back from the bathroom Hannah had sketched a cartoon of Miss Allworth sipping tea. It was absolutely perfect of her. Sunken cheeks and pasted curls. Suddenly I didn't care if Hannah made the group or not. There was something about her I liked.

*   *   *

After we blasted out of the swinging doors past our gold and maroon monitors, we ran all the way home to Hannah's apartment. Tom Cwick yelled after me, "Hey, Sherman, you'll be sorry if you pal with her." Even though he sent me a beautiful fifteen-cent valentine last year, I hated the way he bullied me and everybody else.

On the way home, Hannah said she took violin lessons, wanted to be a conductor, and that she could send her mind travelling thousands of miles around the globe.

I met her family that very first visit. They all spoke English, Russian, and Yiddish very fast, their voices deep and singing, their movements quick and even. They were all light-skinned, black-haired, and loved books and music. Her brother Alex studied piano; Rachmiel wrote poetry and did impersonations of Al Jolson. At four in the afternoon Mrs. Koznoff invited me to eat dinner. Boiled potatoes, herring in sour cream, black bread. Alex poured me hot borscht. He had bright green eyes with dark lashes. Mr. Koznoff drummed on the oilcloth and hummed. He called me "Vovochka" and asked me where my parents came from.

The apartment was still messy from moving in. Mr. Koznoff was painting it a dark wine color that looked like a wine wilderness. The rooms were cluttered with heavy odd furniture, fat short tables with knit doilies, green horsehair sofas with carved legs, and heavy wine-colored drapes. Stuffed cartons of hundreds of brown photographs of the Koznoff's Russian relatives lay in the long hallway.

Hannah pushed me into her bedroom, picked up her violin, and began playing the "Kreutzer Sonata." That was the first time I ever heard a sonata. The melody reminded me of Mamma's cold remedy — warm milk and honey. The room looked almost round and soft. Then I understood what Hannah meant by making her mind travel thousands of miles. Outside, the grey porch and alleyway and the whole city of Chicago melted away with the notes.

When she finished, we looked at the unpacked boxes of books. I'd never seen nor heard of so many strange titles: *The Brothers Karamazov*, *A Streetcar Named Desire*, *The Razor's Edge*, *Gentlemen's Agreement*, *The Three Musketeers*, and a whole series by someone named Sholem Asch.

I picked up a copy of *East River*.

"That's about the Russian Jews who lived in New York in the early days. My grandpa knew the author. It's Mamma's, but you can borrow it. See, it's signed here on the first page."

Suddenly Mr. Koznoff began shouting in Russian. Hannah had to help unpack the books. She gave me *East River*, and I ran down the stairs humming, "Mares Eat Oats."

When I got to the corner Tom Cwick was throwing stones against the lamp post. His leather jacket hunched up around his shoulders nearly touching his D.A.

"Have a cool time at the new kid's?" he snickered.

"Yeah, real cool," I hugged the book tight.

"What she give you? One of her father's Commie books?"

"None of your business."

"You'll be sorry, Sherman. Reading them dirty books."

*   *   *

When I got home, I was too stuffed to eat Mamma's lamb

chops. She was really mad. Then I noticed how boring our furniture looked for the first time, our off-white walls, blond spinet, white satin sofa tucked under plastic covers, tightly drawn venetian blinds. Mamma asked me a lot of questions about the Koznoff family, but I pretended like I didn't know anything.

Papa was in the dining room listening to the McCarthy trials he always listened to on our brand new TV set. "How come the Koznoffs are so different from us if we're both Jewish? What does it mean to be a Communist?"

Papa frowned and stared in the TV set. "I don't know what you're talking about. I suppose whoever these newcomers are, they have another way of looking at life," he said.

"Hannah told me she doesn't go to Sunday School. Her parents don't believe in it."

Again that made Mamma mad. "Denise, why don't you look at Marsha Samuels. *She* goes to Sunday School."

Then Mamma mumbled something to Papa about finding out who this family was and Papa whispered something to Mamma about atheism.

But the more that Mamma and Papa disapproved of my playing with Hannah, the more I ran to her house after school, the more I loved her family and their painted wine wilderness. Mamma said Hannah practiced too much for a twelve-year-old girl, called it an "obsession," which was weird since she hollered I *didn't* practice piano enough. Once when Mamma saw Mr. Koznoff on the street, she turned away and huffed, "He sure knows how to put airs on for a man that's *only* a junk dealer." I wanted to say that *she* put on airs when she played Mah-Jongg with Mrs. Samuels, but I kept still.

Because Mamma's tone made me angry, I decided to finish *East River* even though I didn't like it. When Mamma thought I was asleep, I turned on my night light and read until eleven o'clock. First I glanced through for any love parts, but then I got interested in Moshe Wolf Davidowsky's grocery store, his crippled son, Nathan, and Mary McCarthy, the Irish orphan in love with Nathan. For some reason Mary made me think of Tom.

The next morning I put the book in my briefcase and brought it to school to give back to Hannah. When I arrived a few minutes late, Miss Allworth was already patrolling the aisles. She gave me a nasty look.

"And why are you late, Denise Sherman?"

My heart thumped loudly. I dropped my briefcase on the way," I stammered.

"Perhaps you should clean out your briefcase so it's not so heavy. Let me see it."

I froze on the spot while she waited for me. I knew something terrible was going to happen. She pulled out *East River*.

"Who gave you this to bring to school? I don't believe it belongs to our school library."

I gulped. "Hannah."

As she stood there flipping the pages, I prayed she wouldn't find the part about Irving Davidowsky and Mary McCarthy making out.

Then her face grew red. "Denise, I'm surprised at you. I'll keep this book for now. Begin your English assignment and go on to the unit on Mexico immediately."

Miss Allworth turned to Hannah, who looked right at her. "Hannah, if you were allowed to bring such books to your old school, you are not allowed to bring them to Woodrow Wilson. If this happens again, I'll have to phone your parents."

"But there's nothing *wrong* with *East River*," Hannah balked.

Miss Allworth's eyes grew large. "How dare you talk back! One more remark and I'll phone your father this instant. Class, I must step outside for a moment. Marsha will be monitor. Write down the names of anyone talking or out of his seat."

After Miss Allworth left, Hannah stabbed me in the back with a pencil. She glared at me. "You stoop. Couldn't you tell her something else?"

"I couldn't think of anything. I'm sorry, honest. We better not talk. Marsha's writing down names. I'll buy you a waffle after school, okay?"

"Okay, but I hope Miss Allworth doesn't phone my pa. He can be really strict at times."

Tommy Cwick stood up on his desk and flew a paper kite. "Goody Two-Shoes got in trouble, ha, ha, ha."

Just then Miss Allworth returned carrying *East River* in her hand. She punished the whole class for disorderly conduct with fifty hard decimal problems. But she hadn't phoned Mr. Koznoff that day. She *never* phoned him. She didn't even change our seats. She just kept *East River* until June and then returned it to Hannah without a word. I always wondered if she liked the book.

*　*　*

At three o'clock Amadeo the waffle man waved to us. Black beret, pencil mustache, purple vest and all. We ran across the street to his gold cart, and I bought two hot waffles. When I handed Hannah hers, he murmured something in Italian. I loved when he did that even though I couldn't understand a word. Like when Hannah's parents spoke Russian or Yiddish. My parents knew some Yiddish too, but never spoke it.

Hannah and I stood in the autumn wind watching the leaves swirl. A light drizzle wilted my feather-edge and speckled my new penny loafers.

"Let's go to your house today; I'm getting soaked," she said.

"No, yours is more fun."

"Okay, in a sec." Dumping a mound of sugar on her waffle, she glanced around to see if Tom was still dragging on his cigarette. He leaned against the grey brick walls of the school and puffed away. For a moment Hannah bit her nails with enjoyment. Then she squealed, "Let's beat it!"

We ran up the boulevard past Waxman's Candy Shoppe, Minnie's Laundromat and Walgreen's, where the eighth graders ate French fries and drank cherry cokes. At the intersection of Jackson and Crawford, Tom started gaining on us. "Hey, lamebrains! I wanna talk to you!" he yelled.

"Don't look back!" Hannah warned.

Noses in the air, huddled together we ran past the crossing guard just as the light turned red. Tom stood across the street shouting, "Hey, Sherman, she only pals with you because your father pays for her waffles!"

With a triumphant leap we headed toward Hannah's wine wilderness and dashed upstairs. No one was home. The quiet felt good. We peeled off our socks and warmed our feet on the radiator. Our noses dripped from the chill. When we were dry, Hannah ran into the kitchen and hauled out a box of stale Uneeda Biscuits and a package of Philadelphia Cream Cheese. We carried them to her room, lay down on her bed and began to munch.

"What makes Tom so mean?" I asked.

"I bet his pa drinks."

"How do you know?"

"I saw him coming out of a tavern after my violin lesson."

"Humm. Listen, I'm sorry about the book."

"Forget it. Miss Allworth didn't phone Pa."

"Tell me one thing. Does anyone die at the end?"

"The father."

"Did he go to heaven like he wanted? He always worried about that."

"Are *you* worried about it?"

"Not really."

"Then why do you ask if you know there's no god and no heaven."

"I didn't say that. I'm not *sure* what there is."

"Listen, if there were a god then all those terrible things wouldn't have happened to my family."

I knew she meant the war that ended when I was in first grade, but my parents told me not to talk about it.

She shook her head. "Honestly, don't you know anything? I bet you think storks bring babies, too."

I laughed and munched on my biscuit but didn't answer.

While we were talking, Mrs. Koznoff came in. She wore a long coat and a long flowered dress. She said she'd been to some kind of meeting about somebody named Rosenberg, and had a headache from it. I gulped down my biscuit and thought I'd better leave.

Taking the steps two at a time, I prayed I wouldn't bump into Tom Cwick on the way home. I didn't.

*   *   *

The autumn rains turned to snow. Hannah was absent from school with the flu. I kept glancing at her empty desk every hour. Everything was wrong. I had slipped in decimals, my piano lessons were awful, Marsha Samuels hadn't invited me to the hop she was giving that Friday night.

I trudged home alone through the snow. The soft white cover on the school slide and merry-go-round had turned slushy and grey. Although Amadeo smiled, I didn't stop to buy a waffle. If the bad weather kept up, he wouldn't come around again until spring.

Tom sat in the gutter packing snowballs. "What's the matter, id-kay? No one to play up to now that lover-girl's not here?"

"Oh, shut up."

"Did Samuels invite you to her hop tonight?"

I shook my head.

"Me neither. You and me are the only two she didn't invite—besides you-know-who." He moved closer to me. His eyes were pale blue and his hair smelled of Vitalis. "You know you could be real popular if you didn't hang around with *that* queer. You got cute freckles."

I moved away from him. "Don't call Hannah a 'queer.' She knows more than any kid in this dumb school. Anyway, I don't want to be popular. I don't like the way the popular kids act."

"Yeah? How do they act that's not good enough for you?"

"They act—fast."

"Your friend Hannah is fast. Yeah, Hannah Koznoff is a fast dirty Commie Jew, a kike like them Rosenbergs who are gonna be hanged."

At once the look in his eyes, the sound of the "Kreutzer Sonata," the pages of *East River* all rushed together in my head. For a second I stood there looking at him. Then with all my strength, with tears rolling down my cheeks, I kicked Tom Cwick in the shins. One, two, three times. He froze like a corpse, but he never moved. Then I ran away. As I ran, I could hear Amadeo shouting after me, "*Bravissimo, Denizia, bravissimo!*"

KEEPING SACRED SECRETS

Vickie L. Sears

"It's the way I want it. There doesn't need to be any further discussion."

Mary Ann watched Ginger turn to leave. She saw a lot of her mother's back, a strong slope on a 5'9" frame. Her shoulders were rounds of pale tan with freckledots of pink patches. When Ginger was angry her shoulders would tighten as she pulled her arms together in a chest crossing, and her neck seemed to shorten in withdrawal. She was doing that now as she walked away.

Mary Ann left the house. She flipped her long black braids over her shoulder and lifted her short slim body onto her bicycle. The best way for her to think was to ride her bike. In the brief time she had lived with Ginger, she had learned that it was important for her to leave when her mother was angry. Now just swinging her leg over the bike she began to feel better. She pedaled around the cul-de-sac that was the neighborhood, a horseshoe of brand-new 1950s cinderblock houses. At the end of the cul-de-sac was a small forest. Mary Ann pedaled towards it and began to catalog what she knew about her mother.

Ginger was seventeen when Mary Ann was born, an accident of insemination by the proverbial dark tall stranger, advertised as the perfect mate in women's magazines. Thomas had been in the Navy in a Navy town. They met at a Tommy Dorsey dance. Ginger had never been with a man before but lost herself to his darkness. She got pregnant, Thomas did the honorable. A second child, John, was born ten months after Mary Ann. "If I had known then what I know now. Well, let the past lay," Ginger would often say. When Mary Ann and John were four and three, their parents divorced. The children stayed with Thomas. Mary Ann never knew why. It was one of the many questions she wanted to ask since she had started living with Ginger three weeks ago. Thomas had died. Mary Ann had been sent to Ginger, though John stayed with their Aunt Jenny. Mary Ann didn't know much about her mother. Whenever she had asked Thomas about Ginger, his reply had usually been something like, "She is a good woman. You'll understand sometime. You can ask more when you're older. It's not the right time. Be patient." Elders often gave obscure answers like that so you learned when you were really ready. It was always frustrating. It never seemed enough of an answer. When Mary Ann finally questioned her Grandmother, the old woman would rock in her chair with a headshake saying, "These are things of adults and sad. There is much pain in the story. You will understand later." Mary Ann never asked questions after that. She thought she could ask her father later. Now he was dead.

Everything she thought she had carefully tucked inside herself tilted in her bellypot and burned. She began to cry. At first the tears were cheek rollings of no sound. When she hit the dirt path in the woods she was sobbing loudly. She pedaled deep into the trees and got off her bike. She stepped over some logs to be away from the path. She came to her tree and flopped onto the damp ground. Facing the fallen cedar, she dug her hands into the decaying tree body. It was a host cedar with several smaller trees shooting up into a skyward weave from the moist maroon womb. Mary Ann rubbed her face in the cedar's soft wetness. Felt it crumble on her cheek. Lay in its softness to cry. After a long time she sat up, resting her back against the tree. Looked at her hands. They were covered with cedar strands. She rolled them in her palms, felt her skin suck in the deep redbrowns. Held open her hands. Brought them to her nose. Breathed the cedar. Her father had said that cedar was a medicine and a teacher. If you listened she would tell you stories. Mary Ann put her palms to her ears. Said, "Okay cedar, tell me what my father would. How do I live here?"

Mary Ann sat silent. She could hear kingfisher chatter, robin whistles and leaves falling through branches. Heard wind in the leaves. Heard her heart. She didn't hear anything she thought were answers. She yelled, "I can't! I don't know how to do it! She wants me to be something I'm not. Nobody ever told me how to do that. Damn you, Daddy! Damn you! Damn you!"

Mary Ann hit the earth. In her head she could hear her Grandmother admonishing her in her limited English that women don't need to curse because they are already strong people. She screamed at her Grandmother. "I don't care, you old dummy! You lied to me! You all just went away! You just threw me away!" She sobbed for what seemed a very long time. When her chest was hard with dryness and her eyes almost swollen closed she sat up and pulled out a notebook from the back pocket of her jeans. "Okay, I'm stuck with Ginger. I'd better write down what I know so I can figure things out," she said to herself.

She put her knowns down and headed her list: *Ginger Facts*

> white lady
> very tidy
> twenty-nine years old
> likes world war II and cowboy music
> going to have a baby
> divorced Daddy and maybe didn't like him
> married Tony, who is Italian and Catholic
> she's Catholic
> wants me to be Catholic
> wants me to stop seeing my other family
> wants me to use Tony's last name
> wants me to pretend I'm Italian so other people won't know
> she's divorced
> wants me to call Tony, father

Mary Ann slumped into a sigh. Said to herself, "I sure don't know very much about my mother. Why does she want me to be Italian instead of Indian? What's the big deal anyway? Why's it so important that people don't know she's divorced and that Tony's not my father?"

She tried to remember other things she knew about Ginger. She couldn't think of anything other than that she read *Reader's Digest* and listened to radio shows. Then she thought that maybe her mother didn't know anything about her either. Maybe if they traded information it would be okay for her to stay an Indian. Said aloud, "She'd like it if she just knew more."

Mary Ann sprang to her feet and ran back to her bicycle, leaping over stumps and fallen logs. She raced to her house, jumping from her still-moving bike as she approached the garage door. She had a separate room in the garage, which was attached to the small concrete buildingblock house her mother and stepfather owned. The room and its division from the house were the only things Mary Ann liked about her new living arrangements.

Mary Ann began to search through her drawers looking for treasures from her other family. She put them onto the bed as she found them. Bones for the game. A turtle shell she was going to make into a rattle. Some snake skin for coagulating cuts. A couple of bear claws her father had given her. An antler for hide cleaning. A wing dress for dancing. Leather to be made into pouches or other things. Feathers. Those of the eagle, quail and duck. Decoration and prayer. A beaded bag, a wristband and coin purse she had made. Grandmother had carefully picked the beads with her, teaching her the need for uniformity of size and color. Told her there must be at least one mistake to acknowledge that only the Creator can make things perfectly. Finally, Mary Ann pulled out a long leather bag and placed it on top of the pile.

She stroked the packet. Unbound its drawstring. She pulled out several bundles, carefully unfolding them. They were medicines. Plants and roots she had gone with Grandmother to gather. Something for the lungs. One for drawing away abscesses. A cleansing for fevers. Another for calling good spirits and dispelling sadness. Tobacco for prayers and offerings. Others she couldn't recall the functions of but knew they were important to have. "I'll have to ask Grandmother," she said. With that she stopped. Sat on the bed looking at the gifts. She thought of the medicines as gifts, because gathering was an activity done only with Grandmother, without her brother. Even when she couldn't understand all she was being told because she didn't have enough of the language, Mary Ann felt special in just being with the Old One.

Jerking herself from her thoughts, Mary Ann said to herself, "It doesn't do any good to mope. Mom's gonna be so excited to see my things and know more about my other life she'll give up the idea of pretending I'm Tony's child. Everything's gonna be alright!"

She began to hum. It started to rain. She smiled. She loved the rain. It was the perfect excuse for reading. That was her favorite pastime. Mary Anne went to the door that led from the garage into the kitchen. With her hand on the knob she stopped to suck in a deep breath of excitement. Then burst into the kitchen. "Mother?" she yelled.

Ginger came from the bathroom. "Why aren't you outside playing?"

Mary Ann glanced at the window. "It's raining."

"Oh, so it is. Well, what do you want?"

"I want to show you some neat stuff in my room. Can you come?"

"Alright, but I have a lot of cleaning to do," said Ginger impatiently.

Mary Ann moved to her mother, taking her hand. Ginger pulled away. "I can walk alone, Mary Ann."

"Okay, but come quick." Mary Ann began to bounce backwards in half jumps.

"This is so neat! You're gonna love my stuff, Mom. Close your eyes so it'll be a surprise!"

Ginger smiled softly. "Okay, but open your door so I don't trip."

Mary Ann positioned her mother in the doorway of her room. Her mother closed her eyes. Mary Ann opened the door and led her into the room.

"Okay Mom, open your eyes!"

Ginger looked at the bed and scowled. "What is all this junk, Mary Ann?"

Mary Ann's face went limp. 'Well, this is a bracelet I beaded. These bones are for a gambling game. This is . . ."

Ginger interrupted, "I know what the things are. It's the same voodoo crap that was around me the whole time I was with your father. It's not part of the real world and I won't have it in my house! I just won't! I want it out of here now. I don't care what you do with it, just get it out!"

Suddenly Ginger sprang forward. Mary Ann jumped to avoid being hit, but her mother went to the dresser instead. She began to pull the drawers out, dumping their contents onto the floor.

"How much more of that stuff do you have?" she screamed.

Out tumbled rocks used for healings and ceremonies. Feathers flew into the air, landing at odd places in the room. Her wing dress floated onto the heap. Finally a notebook of stories and the uses of medicines recorded from her Grandmother was thrown onto the bed. Mary Ann grabbed it but Ginger wrenched it from her hands. Mary Ann felt her chest begin to pound. Her mouth got dry. She wanted to snatch the book and run. Ginger was reading her special, most private things.

"Oh God, Mary Ann. What have they filled your head with?" moaned Ginger, her body trembling.

She reached toward her daughter's cheek. Mary Ann cringed. "Those are sacred ways to use plants as medicines. Stories Grandmother told me. That's special, Mom. Please don't hurt that book!"

The words severed softness. Ginger's face darkened with rage. "They're not sacred! It's witchcraft. Myth! Myths are made up things. You have to get that crap out of your mind. These people don't live in the real world. Now get it all into the garbage."

Ginger swept everything to the floor. Then she left the room, slamming the door.

Mary Ann plopped to the floor amid the devastation. She felt very tiny. As small as on the morning she went into her father's bedroom and couldn't wake him. As little as when her Grandmother came and began wailing, "la la la la la la la la la la," on and on through the days while family members arrived for the funeral. The women joined the keening. Men began a drumming. Mary Ann remembered the day of the funeral. A long wooden box had held her father tight, stretched straight. His thin fingers rested on his belly, woven together. His dark woody skin was as dried as brown chalk. Mary Ann wanted to touch him, but filed past with the adults. The box was poised over a long trench. Around it around it they walked, puting into the box things of her father. Neededs. Water. Corn. Wheat. Berries. His moccasins. Pipe. Harmonica. Pencils. Sketchpad. Writing pad. With everything in the coffin, the men brought the lid over and drove nails into place. Each hammer slam echoed as they nailed darkness over her father. It brought a pinched cry to her throat. Mary Ann knew the nightland was a safe and good world, just another step into a different life. But her father was gone.

Mary Ann snapped back to the present by a noise in the house. She was still sitting on the floor, her treasures heaped around her. She thought about her mother's reaction. "She didn't give me a chance to tell her nothing. She just thinks everything is bad. Why? Grandmother wouldn't teach me bad things. Maybe Mom thinks all Indians are bad. But I'm her daughter. If she believes that, she must think I'm bad too. I don't feel bad, but maybe I am." She wondered what her father would say about Ginger throwing away her Indian things. Wondered what Grandmother would tell her to do with the medicines. "How am I gonna live here with no one to talk to? Who's gonna tell me the truth? I don't know her. I can't talk to her."

She pulled her legs into her body and lowered her head over her knees. She couldn't stop crying. She wished her father had taken her with him. "Why didn't he tell me about my mother? Why didn't any of them tell me how to be half-Anglo?"

She jerked into motion when she heard Ginger at the washing machine. From the closet Mary Ann tugged out one of her boxes. She dropped her things in without ceremony. When she came to the plants, Mary Ann stopped. They were so important. Sacred. She stroked the sage and touched her nose to breathe its pungency. Felt it curl around her mind. She heard it say, "Bury us with ceremony. Let us go home." It came as a chant.

Suddenly she knew what to do. Hurriedly she put the rest of the things into the carton.

She took the box outside and tied it onto her bike, tucking a shovel in. Went to the freezer and took a carton of cigarettes her mother kept there. Then she rode to the woods.

In the forest, Mary Ann stood listening for the best place to do the ceremony. She had to be called. She walked. Listened. Looked on the trees and ground. Finally heard a large cedar tree call to her. She talked with the tree. "I'll do everything as best I can." She trudged back to her bicycle to untie the box and shovel and carried them back to the cedar.

First, Mary Ann prayed to know how best to do the ceremony. Went to the creek. Took off her clothes. Submerged herself in the water. Cleansed her mouth with water. Asked that she speak the most honest words she could. Apologized for not knowing all the right ways to do what was needed. Heard, "All you do with a good heart is enough." Dressed and returned to the tree. Prayed again before she plunged the shovel into the soft dark earth at the base of the cedar. She dug until there was a large earth bowl. She took a piece of leather from the box and began to split each cigarette in the carton, pouring the tobacco into the leather lap.

When she was finished, Mary Ann lined the earth bowl with the tobacco. She carefully laid cedar branches over that. They would draw good spirits. Took her wing dress and rubbed it against her cheek. Remembered the dances she'd done in the dress. Said goodbye. She held her turtle shell, tracing its patterns with her fingers, then lowered it into the grave, remembering the triumph she had felt in eating its chewy dark meat in soup. She hadn't liked it much, but had been proud of being given the shell for having caught the turtle.

One by one, Mary Ann slowly deposited her treasures in the earth, saying goodbye to each. She sprinkled in sage for cleansing. Carefully laid sweetgrass to draw good spirits. Softly covered everything with more cedar and tobacco. Four times she walked around the burial site asking strength from each of the directions of the world. She asked that she not stay angry for having to put her things out of her life. Asked that they would go back to the earth as goodness. Asked for help in living in her new home. Covered over the grave. Sat still for some time before making a final prayer and offering tobacco. She thanked the earth. Thanked the tree. Thanked the Creator. Walked away. She was not crying.

When she reached home, Mary Ann stayed in her room until called for supper. At the table Ginger asked, "Did you do as I said?"

"Yes, ma'am."

"Don't call me that!" Ginger said angrily. "You're not in some institution. It's for your own good. You'll feel much better without all of that mumbo jumbo confusing your life."

Ginger reached for her daughter's arm, but Mary Ann pulled away. She looked at her mother, drew a breath and said, "I made up my mind. I'll use his name and I won't tell anybody you're divorced. People can think I'm his kid so you'll be happy. But I won't tell them that I'm Italian. I won't say I'm Indian either unless they ask. Then, if they do, I'm gonna say they have to get the answers from you. I think that's a whole bunch so don't ask for nothin' else. I won't be what you want me to be. I'm already me."

Mary Ann felt her courage ebbing even before her mother put her fork and knife down. She looked at Tony, but he was looking back and forth from her mother to her. Mary Ann wanted to get out of the kitchen and said, "Excuse me, but I'm not hungry," even though she was. She pushed away from the table and ran to her room before Ginger could speak. She heard Tony say, "Fer Crist sake leave the kid alone." She tried to read but couldn't. She sleep drifted into the earth bowl on the wings of her dancing dress.

*　　*　　*

Sixth grade history class brought discussions of manifest destiny and massacres by Indians. Mary Ann didn't protest though she remembered differences in the history her father had taught. She thought her father must have been wrong because books were honest. All the slaughter of the immigrants was written down. Cloakroom concealed she cried. Lamented her father's lies. Worried that she would be recognized as an Indian. She saw no other dark-skinned children at her school. Looked in other history books. Found it all true. There were diaries of pioneer women. The Whitman Massacre. Wagon trains ambushed. Finally she asked her teacher, "Some Indians were good, weren't they?"

"Yes," came the reply. "The Pilgrims would not have survived without the Indians' help. But in the westward movement they had to share and they didn't want to. Also they didn't understand that the migrants didn't want to hurt them. The government wanted to help these people. Reservations were created. They were to help them live where they would not hurt anyone and be safe. They could become civilized. Some people even live on reservations now. It's best."

Mary Ann swallowed down tears she felt filling her eyes. With a half-lowered head, she looked at the white faces of her classmates. It was important that she stay quiet. She thought no one saw her crying. When the bell rang, she tried to run to the bathroom, but was stopped in the hall by three children.

The tallest said, poking a finger, "I always thought you looked funny. You're a little squaw, ain't cha?"

Mary Ann didn't respond.

The other girl said, "You're as dirty as a nigger, you know! Your parents shouldn't even let you in this school!" She pushed Mary Ann backward. Then gave her another shove. Mary Ann turned to walk away and felt the punch of the boy in the group as he hit her mid-back, knocking her down. Her cheek hit the floor, flipping off her glasses. They shattered under someone's foot. She reached for them, wondering what her mother would say. She sat up and began to collect the books splayed around her. People walked past as though she weren't there. The group was gone. Then everyone was gone. Her books back in her arms, Mary Ann just sat. When all the doors were closed she rose and ran out of the building. She rode her bike toward the woods, her legs pumping anger. She couldn't cry or talk. Her brain stopped moving. She lay on the ground a long while.

Once home, timed to her usual arrival, Mary Ann went to her room. Closed the door. She didn't want to face her mother. But soon after she closed the door, there was a knock. Ginger entered. "Why are you in your room?" she asked. "It's beautiful outside."

Mary Ann lowered her head. Held out her glasses. "I broke them."

Ginger sighed. "These are very expensive. How did you do this?"

"They fell off over the banister onto the concrete."

"How could they do that, Mary Ann?"

"I was running. They just did it. I'm sorry. You can take it out of my allowance, Mom."

"Well, we'll talk about that later. You got a call from your Aunt Jenny today. She asked to have you come for some memorial for your father. She feels it's important for you to be there. I don't think it's a good idea, but you can go. I want your promise, though, that if they ask you to participate in any heathen rituals that you won't. I'll pick you up as soon as it's done and I don't want any dawdling. It's tomorrow so you'll have to stay out of school. I want you to go to Mass with me before you go there. Set your alarm for six." Ginger patted Mary Ann's arm. Left the room.

Mary Ann's mind spun. She shoutwhispered, "Hurrah! I'm gonna see my family at a giveaway!"

She began to sing. Suddenly she stopped. "I don't have a ribbon shirt or wing dress or anything else to get ready." She shrugged. "Well, I'll just go in my regular clothes!" After she finally went to bed, the night seemed endless.

Morning Mass with Ginger brought bells demanding apologies, Latin oaths of incense and the slow melt of holy wafer on the mouth roof. After Mass, Ginger said, "Now you're ready to see your other relatives." They drove in silence to her Grandmother's house. Ginger said, "Remember where you belong and you'll be alright." With that, Mary Ann was left in front of her Grandmother's home.

She felt shy approaching the house. Out of place. Knocked on Grandmother's door, remembering the time she wouldn't. Her Grandmother opened the door. A sudden smile curled her cheeks. She scooped the child to her body. Mary Ann stayed in the hug a long time. There was no talking. Grandmother walked, arms enfolding Mary Ann, to her rocking chair. "Sit with me," said the Old One in her tongue. It was good to hear. Comforting just in its sound.

"I'm too big, Tsla," responded Mary Ann in the now unfamiliar language.

"Aaaayy, you are never too large for the lap of a Grandmother. I just change the way you are held. Sit with me."

Carefully, Mary Ann crossed her body over her Grandmother's, dangling her legs across the arm of the rocker. She rested her head on the old woman's sagged breasts. Her Grandmother began to rock while stroking Mary Ann's hair.

"What has happened to your beautiful long hair, little one?" asked her Grandmother.

"It got cut off so I wouldn't look like a 'wild Indian.' I guess it's easier to keep too," Mary Ann answered.

Grandmother was quiet for some time. She began to sing. Mary Ann listened, happy to hear ancient music again from this Elder. Grandmother was good. It didn't matter what the history books read. Finally, Mary Ann said, "I wish I lived with you."

There was silence. Her Grandmother slowly answered, "Your mother comes from a different world with a different God. She does not understand that ways of people can be different and still good."

"Why didn't Daddy and Mom stay together, Grandmother?"

"They were too young. Things were hard with them. He changed in the war. Inside. He got lost. He changed. We did not know him the same. Only the shadows did. Shadows owned him. He got lost and sad. He did not know himself. They did not know each other. They were too different. We all cried."

"It still doesn't make sense. I just want to live with you," said Mary Ann. "Why can't I live with you?"

The Old One's chest heaved up with a hard long breath. She looked down at Mary Ann. "They made a divorce. The paper said, by the law, your mother was too sick of heart to care for you. You should stay with your father. Now your father is in the nightland. You must live with your mother."

Mary Ann protested, "But John lives here."

"Yes. He was made son to your Aunt when your mother was ill."

"Grandmother, make me your child!"

Her Grandmother cupped her hands around Mary Ann's cheeks as her father had done so many times. Mary Ann realized the gesture had been learned from his mother. The woman slowly said, "I will tell truth. Listen well.

"A long time ago Coyote was taking a wood walk when he saw a wagon. It was bumping along the road making dust clouds. He liked them and decided to follow the wagon. He was enjoying the little clouds but not paying much attention and bumped into a bundle which had fallen out of the wagon. He looked in the blanket wrapping and found it was a human baby. He picked the human animal up and ran after the wagon. Although he ran as fast as he could, he couldn't catch the wagon. He sat down for a rest and think. He remembered there was a human animal town to the east so he walked over there. When he was outside the town some of the human animals began to shout and shoot at him.

So Coyote decided to take the human baby home to his wife. Mother Coyote welcomed the human pup, but she worried because she knew that human animals did things differently from Coyote people. But, she raised the human pup anyway. They taught all of the children to hunt, fish, play, and be kind with each other.

Mother Coyote always said that the human pup wasn't as quick at hunting or running because she was different, but she was loved just the same. One day all of the children were playing by a waterhole. All of them except the human pup heard the approaching footsteps of human people. Coyote just barely pushed the pup into a cave before the human people got to the water. As Mother Coyote watched the human people swim and jump and laugh, she saw that they did many things that her human child could not do. She saw that they could not teach her child how to make human talk. She told Coyote that it was time for the human child to learn from human people. The very next day, Coyote and Mother Coyote took their human child to the edge of town. They cried and said, 'You must go now to find some human animal parents to give you your next lessons.' The human child cried too but did as her parents said. And that's just the way it is."

Grandmother stopped rocking. Was silent. Mary Ann tried to see behind the brown irises encircled by yellow. There had to be something different beyond them. But the eyes were steady. They spoke all her Grandmother knew. She laid her head into her Grandmother's chest, nuzzling away her tears. Grandmother rocked.

Later family and friends began to arrive. Food smells filled the house. People circle gathered in the back yard. Gifts were brought and stacked in multi-colored confusion. Mary Ann sat holding hands with her brother. The ceremony took all day with everyone getting to say everything they wanted about what they chose. Toward evening Mary Ann heard her mother's car horn honking. It was insistent. She stacked the things she had been given that day onto the kitchen table. Told her Grandmother why she couldn't take them home. Decided to keep her father's pen and notebook. Said goodbyes and left, not knowing if she would ever see her family again.

She was quiet when she got into the car. Could not look back as they drove away. Didn't want to talk. Thought about facts she had gathered about her mother and father throughout the day. Everything seemed too big to put in order.

Ginger asked, "How was it, Mary Ann?"

She shrugged with "Okay. No big deal."

"Do you want to talk about it?" asked Ginger.

Mary Ann looked at Ginger. Asked herself, "Can I really tell you?" Replied instead, "It was just the usual stuff people do at this sort of thing. It's no big deal."

Ginger snorted in exasperation. "You don't have to be flippant. I was just trying to help."

Mary Ann remained silent. Neither spoke all the way to the house.

At home, Tony asked, "You okay, kid?"

"Yeah," Mary Ann replied, "but I'm tired. Gonna go to sleep. See ya." She patted Tony's arm as she left.

*　*　*

One evening some months later, Ginger asked, "My Lord, Mary Ann! Don't you read anything besides books about saints and Indians? There are so many fascinating things in the world. Like animals. You like animals, don't you? Why get buried in these books?" She tossed one onto the kitchen table. It landed with a thud.

Mary Ann wanted to tell her mother that she was looking for good things about Indians. Instead she said, "I'm going to be an anthropologist so I have to know about these people."

"An anthropologist? I thought you were going to be a doctor," Ginger replied. There was a slight smile on her face.

"Well, yeah, but I'm just interested in a lot of things. I can be anything really. Can't I?"

Ginger grinned and patted Mary Ann's shoulder. "Yes. You can be anything. But please try to read something else too."

Mary Ann looked at her mother. "Mom, can I ask you something about the old days?"

"What, you mean like ancient times or American history?"

"No. I mean about your old days?"

Again Ginger smiled. "Oh, the really ancient times?"

Mary Ann felt puzzled. She smiled the smile she knew she should.

Ginger said, "Well, ask away. If I get too tired from being so old, you know, I'll tell you."

Mary Ann sucked a long breath and asked, "Were you happy when you were married to my father?"

Silence air hung. Then Ginger said, "That's a big question. I'm not sure I can answer it very well. Have you been thinking about this a long time?"

Mary Ann lowered her head and nodded.

"Well, we met in a hurry and got married in a hurry. I thought he was the most handsome man I'd ever met. Of course, I hadn't done much dating, but he would have been hard to resist what with his shyness and quiet ways. He didn't talk about his family much. Except I knew they were really close because they were on the phone all the time. After the war, we came back here. We moved in with his mother. That's when I learned she didn't speak English. Things were different. He spent a lot of time with all of his brothers and sisters. He was always away singing in a drum group. I never understood what was going on. He wouldn't come to Mass with me anymore. People looked at us funny when we went to the movies or the store. They said things.... In California they thought he was Spanish or Mexican. That was alright. Things were very different here. We couldn't talk anymore, that's all. But he was a good man. He had a good heart."

Ginger began to rock in the chair. "Why did you go away and leave me?" asked Mary Ann.

Ginger stared at her. The corners of her mouth pulled back. "Do you have some need to torture me, Mary Ann? These are just plain rude questions."

"I don't mean them to be. I just thought maybe. . . ."

"Well, I didn't just up and leave you kids. Things just got . . . got too big. I just got kind of sick and had to go. . . . I just had to go." Ginger looked away.

Mary Ann said, "I think I know about that, things becoming too big. Sometimes I just go to sleep. Is that sort of what it was like, Mom?"

Ginger was gazing at the wall. She didn't seem to be listening.

"Mom? . . . Mom?"

Ginger slowly turned her head and looked at her. "What now?"

"Could I ask you one more thing, Mom?"

"Alright, but this is all I can take for one night. Okay? If you want to have more answers, when you're sixteen you go read the divorce records. Alright?"

Mary Ann said, "Sure, Mom." She cleared her throat. "Well, if Dad had a good heart and was okay, why isn't it alright for me to do regular things with his family? Why did you take me completely away? Can't I be like them and be with you both?"

Ginger looked confused. She said, "That's too many questions to sort out. I don't want to talk about these things."

She began to rise from the chair. Looked down at Mary Ann. Her face suddenly softened. She put her hand under Mary Ann's chin and shook her head. Sat back in the chair.

"I'm only going to ever say this to you once, Mary Ann. I don't know if I can make you understand. There are so many things in the world that are cruel. People mostly, I guess. Ideas too. But those come out of people. I suppose I don't really know. But there's badness. You and John are different from lots of children. I can't do anything about him now. He will grow up with a lot of strange ideas which won't help him get along in the world. But you. You will be alright. You'll go to a Catholic church, schools just like other kids and be normal. When you were born I promised you things would be alright. I looked in your crib and said, 'You're only half Indian, but I'll make it alright.' You'll be alright. You'll be just like all the other kids. I promise you, Mary Ann. No one will ever say terrible things to you. I promise."

Ginger got up and hugged Mary Ann close to her. Mary Ann could feel her crying. Felt her own tears slide down her cheeks.

Spoke inside her head, "Oh, Mom. I'm already different. It was okay the way it was. It's never going to be how you think it is and you're never going to know, are you?" She closed her eyes and saw Mother Coyote.

SYLVIA

Pamela Painter

THEY WERE SHADOWS, silhouettes, when Lynne opened the door. The man achieved color first, pale pink glazed with a half day's growth of beard. The girl was mixed shades of brown and grey.

Lynne invited them in as the man waved a white paper. "You'll have to sign this first, Miss, and write me a check"—her first week's pay. "I got to get back to the city." He turned to the wall to write out the receipt, ignoring the hall table, keeping an eye on his Cadillac humming in the drive.

The girl placed two shopping bags on the floor in front of her feet and shifted an armful of papers and a worn red dictionary from one arm to another. She watched the bags, waiting.

Lynne went to the kitchen for her checkbook. She had wished for a soft, plump woman of fifty-five, a grandmotherly sort, and now she felt her vision narrow to this slim hard girl of—nineteen.

"We guarantee she'll stay a week. Then it's between you two. Everything O.K., Sylvia?"

Sylvia nodded and looked over her shoulder to the man's car. Lynne gave him the check. Silently they watched him drive away.

For the first time in months Lynne and George lingered over dinner as Sylvia cleaned up in the kitchen. The children called her Black Sylvia for the first two days because they already knew a white Sylvia who lived just three houses and, Lynne thought, one world away.

June 9 1970 today is my birthday and I am thirteen years old and mama has been telling me for so long that i'm a bad girl that I almost feel its true and I want to be a good girl for her but its hard when all the other kids is running out and having fun and mama says it ain't just fun and I guess I know what she means because the last time we scared some whitey on the train she was a little old lady with a face like the underside of pizza dough and I wasn't sure what junebug would do when she only give us thirty-five cents crying and wailing that she didn't have no more and lord have mercy on her soul.

When the Agency check arrived with Lynne's bank statement three weeks later, Sylvia was still there. Still waiting but no longer watching. They had passed the crisis in the second week.

Sylvia had complained about a sore on her back. A red bruise, almost a wound, covered her shoulder blade. "From a mean fight with my sister," Sylvia said. Lynne smoothed some ointment from one of their prescriptions on Sylvia's skin. The white cream became translucent before dissolving into glistening redbrown skin. Then the white gauze and tape symmetrically applied.

Sylvia shrugged her blouse down. "I didn't know if you'd mind touching me or not." Arch smile.

"Oh, Sylvia, of course not." But somehow the sense of rising to the occasion was wrong too. "I'll look at it again in a few days."

Time started sliding by. Nancy Winters often came over from next door to join them for a cup of coffee, and twice she assured Sylvia that some of her best friends were black. Lynne and Sylvia laughed about it when she left. They were in it together.

Soon Lynne returned to her weaving in the early afternoons when Jimmy napped upstairs and Sylvia took David and Susie to the park. She began reading again and if, occasionally, she laid her book aside in helpless anger at the inequality in hers and Sylvia's lives, she inevitably finished every book she started.

Sylvia loved the children and they adored her, arguing about who was going to sit next to her at dinner, and taking turns helping her wash her soft cap of short black hair. She wore her wig only when guests were expected.

Each night as Lynne and Sylvia were putting the children to bed

Sylvia told them a story. Sometimes the stories began with the closing and opening of the bathtub drain, and other times she said that due to circumstances beyond her imagination the story would be continued the following night. They always gave their father a capsule summary of the evening's tale. Molly the mouse. Junebug and the case of the missing month. Allie the slippery eel.

Lynne bought a large notebook and suggested Sylvia write down the stories. The first was seven hundred fifty-three words, Sylvia counted them, with no capital letters and one period at the end. Together they worked on how sentences sound.

"Do you hear it, Sylvia? How my voice drops where a period belongs?"

"It's like music," Sylvia said. Then she told Lynne about the diary. She pulled out a grey folder with her name on the front. The pages were limp and uneven, all in pencil. Lynne weighed it in her hands. "That's a lot of writing."

Sylvia fanned the pages. "Yeah. Maybe you can read it sometime." Then she put it away again, on the top shelf of the closet, out of the children's reach.

Daily Sylvia talked to friends on the South Side. She called them from the breakfast room while she was setting the table and Lynne was fixing dinner. Her musical voice drifted in and out of different sounds as if controlled by organ stops. A different language for another place. Sylvia had been there for two months when the music stopped.

"Shit." The telephone clanged down.

"What's wrong?" Lynne turned around from the stove. Nancy, who had just walked in, raised her eyebrows.

Sylvia slumped into a chair shaking her head. "Allie said word is around I'm going to get smoked if I go back home."

"Smoked?" Nancy repeated, but Lynne knew.

"Shot up." Sylvia wet her lips. "Not dead shot, just enough so it breaks you up a little, or leaves a scar, cripples you maybe."

"But what for, Sylvia?" Lynne took her sauce off the stove and turned down the heat.

"Can't you go to the police?" Nancy asked.

"The po-lice! They're the ones caused the whole thing. You people don't understand about police." She sighed. "Mama always said I'm at the wrong place at the wrong time. Last fall I seen something I wished I hadn't seen and those no-good gals with me ratted to the pigs and then said I told. And now Trainer's in jail and his friends are out looking for me. I gotta get it fixed or I can't go home. I gotta call Willy. He'll make it right." She left to get her red book of telephone numbers.

Nancy shook her head. "Christ, that's all we need. The Young Vice Lords, or whatever they call themselves, marching on Winnetka."

Willy wasn't home. "You tell him call me tonight, that it's important. And don't be giving this number out till you see him, you hear?" She had taken off her wig and was running a hand over her hair.

"What can Willy do?"

"Willy's the High Priest of the Scorpions. The ones I told you about. He's big and mean and if he tells Trainer's friends it wasn't me I'll be O.K. I was up here anyway so how could I have ratted on him?" Logic lulled her features smooth. "But Sharker sure better find Willy tonight."

That evening Sylvia went around with Lynne to check the children and put out the lights as George locked up. Lynne heard her recheck the backdoor five minutes later. The phone rang at two o'clock. George answered. "It's for Sylvia, for God's sake. Hell of a time to call."

When Sylvia didn't respond to Lynne's knocking, Lynne opened her door and gently pushed at her shoulder.

"Sylvia," she called softly.

The sheet flew back from her long arms and Sylvia cringed against the wall, eyes wide.

"Sylvia, it's only me. There's a phone call for you."

Lynne waited in the dark kitchen till Sylvia finished talking. They met at the steps.

"That was Willy. He's seeing Trainer's friends tomorrow to clear it up."

Lynne nodded.

"He's calling back tomorrow after he sees them. Then he's going to get them gals who did the lying."

"Well, you'll sleep better now," Lynne said. And for her, later, the justice was done in an alley she couldn't remember ever seeing, against a brick wall where two girls stood, faceless, and then she smelled something burning and felt like she couldn't breathe till George woke her saying, "Lynne, Lynne. You must be dreaming."

Two days later Sylvia said Willy had taken care of everything.

April 17 1972 it's called the audy home and I been rotting in solitary for three days and I can tell from the start I ain't going to like this place cause when I saw the other gals at supper for the first time I knew being tough is the only thing that's going to keep me alive since everything i've heard about this place looks to be as true as my mama says it was and the smell and the roaches are getting into my clothes and at supper I got a look on my face that said don't fuck with me baby and after the queen tried to take my bread and I give her the elbow she let me alone for now but that ain't saying it ain't going to get a whole lot worse before it gets better.

Throughout the summer Sylvia worked for five days and went home on weekends. Mornings were spent washing and folding clothes, running the vacuum. Lynne and Sylvia together. Afternoons were interludes at the beach and parks. By the end of July Sylvia announced she had written twenty-three stories.

But it was too hot in Chicago.

A man, first thought to be an animal, was found skinned and cut up in a garbage can two blocks from Sylvia's apartment. Sylvia knew him. "Ben, he was a bad one. I knew he'd get it some day but no one deserves to die that way like an alley cat that screams once too many times."

"Dying is sacred," Lynne said and her words were cool with children playing outside in the sand, not hot with heated streets and dying vegetables.

"Mrs. Hollander," Sylvia said. "There's something I want to tell you about."

Lynne stiffened, waiting for that other world to blur the edges of her own. She loved Sylvia here in Winnetka, she hadn't known her in another place. Sunlight warmed the folded clothes on the table between them, just washed and dried. Sylvia unfolded one of David's shirts.

"Do you remember that old woman in Evanston that was killed a year ago?"

Lynne shook her head 'no' before the answer came.

"Well that was pinned on me."

"Sylvia!" They looked at each other across the table.

"I was there like Mama says in the wrong place at the wrong time. I didn't do it but I spent time in jail and I sure know I ain't never going back."

And then she remembered the headlines. An elderly woman and her sister in a Volkswagen had pulled to the curb and were told to hand over their purses, which they refused to do, and *the driver was killed*. Then there followed an account of a wild chase down Lake Shore Drive to the South Side until the car ran out of gas and they were caught and Lynne thought Who? Sylvia? Our Sylvia?

"Oh, Sylvia." She didn't know what to say.

"I was in the car with Skye, he's the one that shot her, there were four of us, three guys and me, and another car with Allie in it but they got away and when they hauled us in them three decided to hang it on me and they almost got me put away but some lawyer knew I didn't do it and he got me off. The woman's sister told them it wasn't me."

"But what happened to the one that did it?"

Sylvia shrugged. "Skye, he got off too. Even after the lady put the finger on him. She knew him. But the lawyers got her confused. That's what happens most of the time. That's why the cops drag us to the lake and work us over instead of taking us in to the station-house."

Outside the window, Susie and Jimmy and David were all in the sandbox now, each with his own bucket and shovel and corner and Jimmy was sifting sand for small stones and leaves to be tossed over the side onto the grass.

Sylvia refolded David's shirt. "I had to tell you. I can't sleep with the nightmares and knowing you didn't know, seeing it painted on my eyelids with my head on your pillow and the kids asleep upstairs."

Lynne sighed and smoothed the soft towels in front of her. There had almost been too much said for her to hold it all.

"I guess I want to know if I can stay." Her brown hands

smoothed the white clothes. From the back yard came the muted cries of children playing in the sun. Sylvia. Here in Winnetka.

"I'm glad you told me. I'm shocked as I guess you can tell." She stopped to control her voice, relax her throat. "But I'll get over it. Of course you can stay. Why should you go?"

Sylvia nodded, still looking down. "I like it here. Quiet. Like a hospital zone in the city. It's different. Like how I even got this job. We were just in that agency watching T.V. cause it was raining out and Willy's car had a flat tire and the agency man asked if anyone wanted a job for a few weeks. You should see where my sisters and brothers go to school. Even the colors are different. Nothing's green in the city."

"You're here now," Lynne said firmly. But where, really, is that? she had to add to herself.

September 7 1973 today is the start of my second week back home and it sure feels great even if we are three to a bed with an occasional rat bridging us to the table and I was trying to be a good girl and staying away from junebug and allie and all them cats with their drugs and booze cause I promised mama when she came to the home to get me and cried all over her good black dress and said why wasn't I like my older sisters who never got in no more trouble than just having babies which hurt me a lot cause after I was fourteen and raped bad when the doctor said I can't never have babies and that's what I'd love more than anything in the whole world a little tiny baby and then when junebug said they had some special stuff I told mama I was staying after school to help the teacher cover books and took off over to the vacant lot on tenth street where they were waiting for me and allie and they said true cause it was fine grass and the ride smoother and higher than I've ever been and when I got home I said I didn't feel well and went to bed and watched the moon bend the city into stars and then I cried for mama for she didn't know and I couldn't tell her and I loved her and the moon and the stars and only they knew what my night was like.

And so Sylvia stayed. George said, "Christ, I know what the city's like, I'm there every day. Let her stay." Molly the mouse had children—ten. Junebug discovered a new planet next to Mars which had stolen the missing month. Allie the eel was learning to read. But just when Sylvia seemed to be absorbed into their lives, Lynne could see her soul slowly collect itself together, she could see her begin to long for the hot streets and sidewalk talk, the tense moment in the loose, long stride.

One Saturday morning on their way to the beach, they dropped Sylvia at the train. It was her first visit home in a month and she checked the train schedule every two minutes till she heard it coming down the track. She waved, running away from them, promising to bring back candy for the children. She was wearing Lynne's yellow shirt and she looked good.

Monday the call came. Sylvia's mother.

"Mrs. Hollander? I'm calling from the hospital for Sylvia cause she can't talk. They won't let her talk to you or anyone."

"What happened?" Lynne frantically looked around for a pencil. "Where are you?"

"She ain't hurt bad. She be out in two days but they're taking her to jail first and I got to post bond and I don't have no money for that when there's another baby on the way needing clothes, and my youngest sickly all the time so Sylvia said to ask you. She talks about you a lot. It ain't her fault. She fainted on the steps outside the apartment and cut her head open and the neighbors got scared when they seen all the blood and called the ambulance and the police came too and heard my Sylvia mumbling about a gun in some drawer that she'd bought me and they went into my rooms and took it and now they won't let her out unless I pay them a hundred dollars bond money. Can you help me, Mrs. Hollander? Sylvia says you'll help, but if you can't that's all right too. I keep telling her to be a good girl."

"When do you need the money and where do we take it? My husband—somebody will bring it down." Lynne shook her head as Sylvia's mother said she'd put the police matron on the phone for the address. Lynne heard a firm "Hello."

"You're . . ."

"I'm just the matron in charge here."

"What's going to happen?"

"I don't know anything about the case. Call the station if you want to know what happened. She ain't bad off for the fall she took. Her mother's been here all the time."

"You're by her bed now. Tell Sylvia I said . . . tell her I said we'll help her. Not to worry."

"I'll tell her. And like I said, you better call the station."

Lynne wrote the address of the hospital on the top of the morning paper. Then she sat there with her head in her hands, not wanting to call—for Sylvia. But needing to know. She washed the breakfast dishes and made the beds before she dialed information. For the station.

"Captain Stonier here."

"Hello. This is Mrs. Hollander. I am calling from Winnetka about a girl who works for me. Sylvia Marsden. She's being held on some charges."

"Lemme get the books. Sylvia Marsden. Sylvia Marsden. Here it is. Booked on Sunday at three p.m. Suspected of a heavy dose of drugs. Carrying an unregistered firearm. Loaded."

"Carrying the gun?"

"It was in her purse. She's a bad one, we got a long list on her."

"But she's been working for me and has never . . ."

"Lady, you got to be kidding . . ."

"But I know her . . ."

"And I'm telling you: get rid of her. We got trouble enough."

Lynne waited, pacing the kitchen for her husband to come home. The children, as if sensing something wrong, played together without fighting. Built forts in the playroom, quietly asked for crackers, juice. Asked when Sylvia was coming back.

He, too, knew immediately when she met him at the door. The toys strewn around the house. The absence of Sylvia's voice. Her own face. Tensely she told him the facts. Both versions. He called the hospital and told Sylvia's mother he'd be at the courthouse Wednesday with the money. Lynne's throat ached to talk about it. But there wasn't anything to say, yet. Together they put the children into bed. George read them *Goodnight Moon* while she cried quietly in the livingroom.

The next day George came home an hour earlier than usual. He took off his tie. Loosened his collar. "I got there too late. The judge called her up early and let her out on her personal recognizance.

She left word with a woman in her cell that she was glad we were willing to help her, that she'd be calling you soon."

His last words had been in the air before he'd said them and she knew that if the call came this moment that her voice would fail her, that what she had to say, offer, do, wasn't anywhere her mind could focus on. Only the questions.

"What do I say?" Lynne asked, holding out her hands as if to cradle some fragile answer. "Should we have her back?"

"Christ, I don't know, Lynne. After today. I just don't know. Down there it's a different world." His voice was tired, empty. "It's up to you. Whatever you decide."

And then, two days later, her call:

"Mrs. Hollander. I'm out."

"Sylvia. How *are* you? Your face."

"Oh, I'm all right. It don't show and the stitches kept it good and tight." A pause. "What are the kids doing?"

"They're out in the yard spreading more sand around." Lynne could see them, each in his own territory, building castles, roads that would never touch.

"I'll bet they got most of it in their hair. I sure miss them."

"They miss you too. We all do. They said my stories aren't as good as yours. Even the books."

"I have to go back to court next month. On a Thursday. But I could work that Monday before, to make up for it."

"What happened when you went home, Sylvia?" Lynne closed her eyes but they were too full already and soon the receiver slid wet against her cheek.

"Didn't Mama tell you? I guess I fainted. The neighbors called the ambulance and I must have been saying some wild things about a gun cause they broke into Mama's rooms and found the gun Junebug just give me. And then they booked me."

"What does that mean?" Lynne asked.

"I don't know. Mama said she'd get a lawyer and go to court with me. Even if it goes wrong I'd just get suspended." Sylvia's voice pleaded.

"Sylvia, we've decided not to have anyone helping us out for a while. Maybe in a few months." *And it was done.*

"Mrs. Hollander, you don't think I would have brought that

gun back around those children do you?"

"Oh, Sylvia. I know you wouldn't have. It's just that for a while we've decided to manage, not to spend the extra money." She knew Sylvia was crying in the silence.

"I know what you're saying, Mrs. Hollander. It's all right. I understand."

"I'm sorry, Sylvia." A pause. "Let us know what you're doing. We'd love hearing from you."

"Yeah, I'll call you sometime. I will."

"Mr. Hollander will bring your things down in the next few days to save you a trip."

"Say goodbye to the kids for me, will you? Keep some of my stories for them if you can read my writing. And tell them goodbye."

"Yes, I'll tell them. Goodbye, Sylvia. Take care."

And barely audible, "Goodbye."

The diary was still there. The pages kept blurring as she read. It took her four hours to finish three hundred and some odd pages of penciled script.

February 3 1974 I knew I shouldn't have gone when them two cars pulled up to the curb and allie she yelled for me to come along that they was going for a ride in whitey's town and I had promised mama I wouldn't get in no more trouble but there was this cool dude driving and he was looking at me like he knowed what turns me on and I thought just let him try so I went and got in the car with the driver called spade and he handed me a joint and looked me over again close up real cool and I was thinking that the real fun was coming later when spade's hand on my knee would be higher and round and I'd be laying down instead of sitting up straight as his hand stayed still and gentle and then somehow I was on that wild ride home missing cars and people I thought we'd get killed we was going so fast and then funny-like just a few sputters and we was stopped and Skye threw the gun out of the car so they'd know we wouldn't put up a fight and then they took us in them three dudes and me and they put me in the women's part and I didn't have no paper for days and then when the matron finally gave me some the lawyer said I better not go writing anything that would

get me in more trouble so I put my thoughts away and just concen-
trated on hating that matron who shaved my head and cut my food
in half everytime she felt like letting me know that I was a nigger
and she wasn't and how I knew that if I could kill anyone it would
be her instead of that lady's sister cause she was nice for all she was
a whitey and it was her that let them know I didn't do it and all I
can hear when I see her is her screaming when her sister was shot
and hanging on the steering wheel which gave off a big honk that
went away leaving her wailing that wouldn't she just speak once
but I could tell even from where I was hunched up in the back of
the car that her sister wasn't ever going to call no black a dirty
nigger ever again.

They all missed Sylvia, even the summer seemed to follow her away. Lynne's voice was strong, not gentle, after she put the loom aside. They were five at the table now, their music thinner as if a chord had changed. Books were put back on the shelf. Unswept sand crunched underfoot in the kitchen. In the yards weeds seemed to find their own water from the dry days.

One day in early September Lynne knelt, grooming the flowers, refereeing the children's play. She pushed her hair back with her arm. She was thirsty.

Just as she came in from the garden she saw the battered car stop in the street in front of their house. Three black boys, men, sat talking. Names rang in her ears: Junebug, Willie, Sharker, Spade, Trainer, Skye. She was pulling, tearing off her gloves when the doorbell rang. Susie and David were in the back yard and only Jimmy was in the house with her. Upstairs. All those steps. From the diningroom she could see him looking in. Which one was it? She crept softly through the back hall, then up the stairs to the nursery. She was lifting Jimmy from his crib as the doorbell rang again. Then, holding Jimmy tight against her stomach, his wet diaper soaking through her dress, she ran back downstairs, through the hall, her hand on Jimmy's mouth. He was still there. Big, black. She edged through the kitchen and out the back door. Pushing David, pulling Susie, she dragged them through the hedge to Nancy's house. She didn't look back as she pushed them in and slammed the door. She leaned against the kitchen table. Jimmy still held on to her dress, crying. Susie started to cry, backing away from her. Through the hallway she saw Nancy closing the front door. "Lock it, lock it," she cried as Nancy stared and then ran toward her. Then David was crying too and she was telling Nancy, "Sylvia's friends. They're at my house. Call George."

Nancy pulled Susie and David to her, saying fiercely, "Christ, Lynne, get hold of yourself. They were just selling magazines." And Lynne didn't hear anymore. *Sylvia. Sylvia.* Her world caught in her throat.

WHO SAID WE ALL
HAVE TO TALK ALIKE

Wilma Elizabeth McDaniel

WHO KNOWS HOW Neffie Pike's speech pattern was formed? Her Ozark family had talked the same way for generations. They added an "r" to many words that did not contain that letter. In spite of this, or because of it, their speech was clear and colorful and to the point. Most people understood what they were talking about, exactly.

Neffie was her parent's daughter. She called a toilet, "torelet," and a woman, "worman," very comfortably. The teacher at the country school never attempted to change Neffie's manner of speaking. She said that Neffie had a fine imagination and should never allow anyone to squelch it. In fact, Neffie never really knew that she talked different from most other people.

People in the tiny community of Snowball really loved Neffie. She was a good neighbor, unfailingly cheerful and helpful. The appearance of her tall and boney figure at the door of a sickroom or a bereaved family meant comfort and succor. A great woman, everyone in Snowball agreed.

She would have probably lived her life out in the same lumber house if her husband had not died. In the months that followed his death she developed a restless feeling. Home chores, church and charity work did not seem to be enough to occupy her mind. She started to read big town newspapers at the library in nearby Marshall, something new for her. She became especially interested in the out of state employment want ads. She mentioned to neighbors,

"They are a lot of good jobs out there in the world."

One day she came home from Marshall and stopped at old Grandma Meade's house. She sat down in a canebottom chair and announced, "I have got me a job in California. I am a selling my house and lot to a couple of retired people from Little Rock. They will be moving in the first of June."

Grandma Meade sat in shocked silence for several seconds, then said, "Honey, I do not believe it. I mean that I never in the world imagined that you would consider leaving Snowball. You and Lollis was so happy together here." Her voice trailed off, "Of course nobody could foretell the Lord would call him so young."

Neffie looked stonily at her and said with her usual clarity, "A widder woman is a free woman, especially if she don't have no children. She ought to be free to come and go like she pleases. After all, I am only fifty-one years old. I can do as much work as I ever did. This job is taking care of two little girls while their mother works at some high paying job. She has already sent me a bus ticket. I would be a fool not to go. Everyone has been to California except me. I always hankered to see the state for myself. Now is my chance to see some of the rest of the world. It may sound foolish, but it will sort of be like having a dorter of my own and grand-children. I aim to write you a long letter when I get settled down out there."

Neffie left for California on schedule. After two weeks Grandma Meade began to worry a bit. She said, "I thought that Neffie surely would have dropped us a line by now. The last thing she told me was that she would write me a long letter. Well, maybe she hasn't got settled down yet."

A month passed without any word from Neffie.

Bug Harrison was at Grandma Meade's house when Neffie returned the day after Snowball's big Fourth of July celebration.

Neffie put her suitcases down and began at the beginning. "Grandma, you was so right about so many things. I knowed I was in trouble hock-deep, only one minute after I stepped off that bus in California. A purty young woman come forward to meet me and said she was Beryl. I busted out and told her, 'My, you are a purty worman, even purtier than your pitcher.' She kinda shrunk back and looked at me like I had used a cussword. She stood there holding her little girls' hands and asked me, where on earth did you hear a word like worman, was it a female worm of some kind? She said, 'Worman is woe-man,' like you say woh to a horse.

"Her remark nearly knocked me off my feet. I felt like a fool, and I didn't even know why. My stomach started churning. I durst not say anything to defend myself, because I hadn't done anything wrong.

"We started walking to Beryl's station wagon in the parking lot. I told her that I never was blessed with a dorter or son, either. That set her off again. She said that her children were at a very impressionable age, that I would have to watch my speech and learn the correct pronunciation of words. She did not want them picking up incorrect speech patterns and something she called coll-oke-ism, something I had, and didn't even realize. I decided to shut up and get in the car. The worman had already paid for my fare. I felt that I had to at least give her a few months' service, if I could stand the punishment at all.

"On our way to Beryl's house, she stopped at a drive-in restaurant and ordered cheeseburgers and milkshakes for all of us. I decided to just eat and listen.

"It was sure a pleasurable drive on to Beryl's home. We followed the same county highway for the entire seven miles. The road was lined on both sides with pams, tall with them fronds waving in the breeze. It reminded me of pitchers I have seen of The Holy Land, really touched my heart. I forgot myself again and said that I never had seen pams before except in pitchers. Quick as a flash Beryl told me, 'They are pall-ms, not pams. There is an l in the word.' After that, I sure buttoned up my mouth. I just said yes or no to anything she asked me.

"Her house turned out to be a real nice place, bright and modern with every type of electrical gadget you could think of. There were four bedrooms, each with a bath. I was so tired and upset over Beryl's attitude that I begged off sitting up to visit with her and the little girls. I ran me a full tub of warm water and took me a long soaking bath. I fell into bed and went sound asleep. Worman, I plumb died away, slept all night without waking up. To show you how hard I slept, there was a fairly severe earthquake in the central part of California where Beryl lived. It even shook a few things off a living room shelf. I tell you, I wouldn't have heard Gabriel blow his horn that night.

"I woke up feeling relieved that it was Monday. Beryl left for work promptly at seven-thirty. That meant the girls and I had the house to ourselves. Worman, I am a telling you, they was two living dolls, Pat and Penny. I made them bran muffins for breakfast and scrambled some eggs. They ate until they nearly foundered. It seemed like they had never seen a bran muffin before, asked me if I would cook them the same thing each day.

"I told them I knew how to cook other good old homely dishes, too. Every day, I tried something new on them, biscuits and sausage and milk gravy, buttermilk pancakes, waffles, popovers, french toast, corn dodgers, fried mush. You name it, worman, I cooked it for those dolls. It wouldn't be no big deal for the kids here in Snowball, they was raised to eat like that, but it was hog heaven to Pat and Penny."

Grandma Meade had been listening intently, her eyes pinned on Neffie's face. Now she asked, "How did Beryl like your cooking?"

Neffie laughed heartily. She said, "To put it plain, she LOVED it. I can say that she never found any flaw in my cooking, only made one complaint connected with it. I boirled her a fine big cabbage and hamhock dinner and made cornbread for our supper one evening. When we started to sit down at the table, I said that it was a nice change to have a boirled dinner now and then. That set her off like a firecracker. She said, 'That is boil-ed, not boirled.' I decided to let that snide remark pass. I saw she started dishing up the food—she lit in on it like a starving hounddog. That showed what she thought of my cooking, didn't it? My cooking sure helped me get through them weeks as good as I did."

Bug Harrison broke in, "What were your duties during the day?"

Neffie said, "I was hired to take care of the two little girls. That is what I done. I cooked because people have to eat. I always have, always will. That didn't put no extra strain on me. The girls and I played the most of the day. They would sit on each arm of my chair and listen to me tell them about my life back in Arkansas. I didn't hold back nothing. I told them about haunted houses, ghosts, robbers, bank holdups, tornadoes, snakes, tarantulas, times when the river flooded and we had to float on a rooftop to save our lives. Lordy, worman, they just ate it up. They would listen to me with their eyes as big as saucers. I don't quite know why I done it, but I asked the girls not to tell their mother about my stories. They were as secretive as little private detectives until a week ago. They got so excited over one of my stories that they forgot theirselves. I was busy in the kitchen putting some homemade noodles into a pot of chicken broth. I heard Pat tell her mother, 'Mom, back in Arkansas where Neffie used to live, they are wormans that can tell fortunes for people. They can look right through your face and tell if you are telling the truth or a lie. They can rub your warts with skunk oirl and say some words and all the warts will fall off, never ever come back.' I figured I was in bad trouble, but I kept on dropping the noodles into the broth. I was a hundred percent right about the trouble.

"Beryl blowed her stack. She marched right back to the kitchen with the girls at her heels. She stood in the door and said, 'I have been afraid of this very thing. Neffie, I just can't keep you on any longer.'

"At that point Pat and Penny throwed themselves down on the floor and started bawling like two young calves. Pat sobbed out real angry-like, 'Yes, you CAN keep Neffie! She is the best storyteller in the whole world and the best cooker. If she goes home to Arkansas, we won't never have no more biscuits and sausage and gravy.' The tears began to run down her little face.

"Beryl stood there with her face like a flintrock. It looked like she wanted to be nice to me, but that her duty come first with her. She drawed in her breath and said, 'Neffie, you are as good and kind and honest as you can be, exceptional, but your speech is totally unacceptable. My children are at a very impressionable age. I have tried to overlook it, but they are definitely being influenced in the wrong direction. They say dorter and orter with regularity. This pattern must be eradicated immediately. I shall be happy to pay your traveling expenses home. You can look on this trip out West as my vacation gift to you.' I could see that her mind was made up and she wasn't going to change it.

"I did think to ask her if she had some other babysitter in mind. I didn't want to run out and leave her in a bind without one. She said there was a young girl from the college who wanted day work, so she could attend night classes. She thought that would work out great. I got her point. The college girl would be different from me, more to suit Beryl.

"Well, to shorten my story, she bought me a big box of real expensive chocolates and put me on the bus with my paid ticket, just like she had promised. She and the girls stood there beside the bus waiting for it to pull out. Penny looked up at me and blew me a kiss. I heard her say as plain as plain could be, 'Neffie, you are a sweet worman.' Then I saw Beryl put her hand over Penny's mouth. Right then, the bus pulled out of the depot and I lost sight of them.

"Worman, I done a lot of thinking as that bus rolled along the highway. I would eat a chocolate and think over my experience with Beryl. Things kind of cleared up in my mind, like having blinders taken off of my eyes. I saw I had really been ignorant of some things that other folks knowed. I didn't talk right to suit some of them, but that wasn't my fault. *I didn't know we was all supposed to talk the same way.* I thought people hadn't all talked the same since before God tore down their tower at Babel and confused all their tongues. Folks all over the world have talked different ever since then. I guess some of them like Beryl want to go back to pre-Babel days. Anyway, it was sure an eye-opener to me, hurt me, too. Beryl just plain separated herself from me. It was like she took a sharp knife and cut a melon in half, and throwed away the half that was me. You know what you do with a piece of melon you don't want. You throw it with the rinds into the garbage can. Worman, who said that we all have to talk alike? Can anyone tell me that?"

SISTERS

BarbaraNeely

> *. . . and are we not one*
> *daughter of the same dark mother's child*
> *breathing one breath from a multitude of mouths . . .*
> from the Sisterhood Song of the Yenga Nation

THE OFFICES OF Carstairs and Carstairs Management Consultants had that hushed, forbidden air of after five o'clock. No light shone from beneath any of the office doors bordering the central typing pool which was also deserted, except for the new cleaning woman working her way among the desks. Lorisa was the last of the office staff to leave. She'd pushed the button for the elevator before she remembered the notes on Wider Housewares she wanted to look over before tomorrow morning's meeting. She turned and took a shortcut through the typing pool to her office.

"Good evening," she said to the grey uniform-clad back of the cleaning woman as the woman reached down to pick up a wastebasket. Lorisa automatically put on her polite, remote smile, the one that matched the distance in her tone, while she waited for the woman to move out of her way.

Jackie turned with the wastebasket still in her hand and let her eyes roam so slowly over the woman who'd spoken to her that she might have been looking for something in particular. Then she nodded, briefly, curtly, before turning, lifting the basket and dashing its contents into the rolling bin she pushed along ahead of her. Only then did she step aside.

Lorisa hurried into her office, careful not to slam the door and show her irritation. Where did they find the cleaning staff, the asylum for the criminally insane? The woman had given her a look cold enough to cut stone and barely acknowledged her greeting— as though she were not worth the time it took to be pleasant. She, who was always careful to speak to the gum-chewing black girls who worked in the mail room, the old man who shined shoes in the lobby, the newspaper man and any other of her people she met in the building who did menial work. None of them had ever been anything but equally polite to her. She had noticed the shoeshine man always had something pleasant to say to the mailroom girls and only a "Good day" to her. But considering the difference in their positions, his reticence with her seemed only natural and nothing like the attitude of the cleaning woman.

Although she'd only returned for her notes, she found herself moving papers from one side of her desk to the other, making a list of small tasks for tomorrow, staving off the moment when she would have to confront the cleaning woman once again. But Lorisa realized it wasn't the woman's curt nod or the slowness with which she'd moved aside that made her reluctant to leave her office. It was those eyes. Big, black, dense eyes with something knowing in them—something that had made her feel as though her loneliness and her fear of it, her growing uneasiness about her job, the disturbing hollowness where pleasure in her comfortable life should be, and all her other fears and flaws were as visible to the cleaning woman as so many wrinkles and smudges on her dress. When their eyes had met, the sense of secret knowledge already shared had filled her with an almost overwhelming desire to say something, to explain something about a part of herself she couldn't name. The woman's look of cold disdain had only corroborated her feeling of having been revealed and found wanting. "Your shit ain't so hot, honey, and you know it," the woman's eyes seemed to say. It didn't occur to Lorisa that the way she'd spoken to the cleaning woman could have anything to do with the woman's response. She was tired, with too much work and too little rest. And she was always over-imaginative when her period was about to start. She forced herself to open the door to her office and was nearly lightheaded with relief to find the cleaning woman nowhere in sight.

In the descending elevator, she realized that the term "cleaning woman" rang false against the face and figure she'd just encountered. Cleaning women were fat and full of quiet kindness and mother wit. They were not women who looked to be in their late twenties—her own age—with faces strong and proud as her own. They didn't have lean, hard-muscled arms and eyes like onyx marbles. She remembered her grandmother, her father's squat, black, broad-nosed mother who had cooked and cleaned for white people all of her life. On those rare occasions when Lorisa's mother had consented to a visit from her mother-in-law, or, rarer still, when the family paid the older woman a visit in North Carolina, Grandmother would wait on everyone. She would slip into your room while you were in the bathroom in the morning and make your bed, hang up your clothes, and spirit away anything that looked the least bit in need of mending, washing, or pressing. But her dedication didn't earn her much praise.

"Young black girls learn enough about being mammies without your mother to set an example," Lorisa had once heard her mother say to her father. Her mother was explaining why it was impossible for Lorisa to spend part of her summer with her grandmother, despite Lorisa's and her grandmother's wishes. She'd been sent to camp instead, a camp at which, she remembered now, the white kids had called her and the three other black girls "niggers" and put spiders in their beds. As she crossed the lobby, it occurred to her that her grandmother had once been young, just like the woman cleaning the typing pool. Had there been fire in her grandmother's eyes, too, when she was young? Had she spit in the white folks soup, the way the slaves used to do? How long did it take to make a *real* cleaning woman?

* * *

Jackie banged another wastebasket against her bin with such vigor she left a dent in the basket. What had made her act like that? She slammed the basket down beside the desk and moved on to the next one. The woman was only trying to be polite. But a mean, evil rage had risen up at the very sight of her—walking around like she owned the place, having her own office. And those shoes! She must have paid a hundred dollars for them shoes! Who'd she think she was? Jackie dumped the last basket and began dry mopping the floor with an over-sized dustmop. A college education didn't give her the right to give nobody that uptight little greeting, like an icicle down somebody's back, she thought. She'd run into three or four other black women with really good jobs in other buildings where she cleaned. A couple of them had had that air of doing you a favor when they spoke to you, too. But they'd been light-skinned and looked like models, which somehow made their hinctiness less personal. This woman's smooth dark face and big round eyes reminded Jackie of a girl she'd hung out with in school; and she had a cousin with the same big legs and small waist. She didn't need for no plain ole everyday-looking black woman to speak to her because she thought she ought to. She got more than enough of being practically patted on her head, if not her behind, from the phony whites she worked for. She wasn't taking that stuff from one of her own, too!

She let her mind slip into a replay of her latest run-in with her snooty white supervisor in which she'd once again had to point out that she only gave respect when she got it. She was hoping to draw a parallel between the two situations and thereby relieve herself of the knowledge that in the moment when she'd first seen the woman standing there—as crisp and unused as a new dollar bill, as far removed from emptying other people's wastebaskets as a black woman was likely to get—she had been struck dumb by jealousy. She swung the mop in wide arcs, putting more energy into the chore than was called for.

She was just finishing up the Men's Room when she heard the elevator bell. When she left the bathroom no light showed from beneath the woman's door. Although she'd already cleaned the private offices, Jackie crossed the typing pool and tiptoed into the woman's office. She stood in the middle of the room. Light from the street below made turning on the overhead light unnecessary. A hint of some peppery perfume lingered in the air, like a shadow of the woman who worked there. It was a good-sized office, with a beige leather sofa under an abstract painting in shades of blues and brown; a glass and chrome coffee table with dried flowers in a bowl. A big, shiny, wooden desk.

Jackie ran her fingers along the edge of the desk as she walked slowly round it. She stood in front of the leather desk chair and placed the fingertips of both hands lightly on the desk. She leaned forward and looked toward the sofa as though addressing an invisible client or underling. Then she sat—not as she usually sat, with a sigh of relief at getting off her feet as she plopped solidly down. She sat slowly, her head held high, her back straight. In her imagination, she wore Lorisa's raw silk shirtwaist and turquoise beads. Gold glistened at her ears and on her small, manicured hands. Her hair was long and pulled back into a sleek chignon. The desk hid her suddenly corn-free feet, sporting one hundred dollar shoes. And she knew things—math, the meaning of big words, what to tell other people to do . . . things that meant you were closer to being the boss than to being bossed.

Once, so long ago it seemed like the beginning of time, she'd thought she might be something—nothing grand enough for an office like this. Being a secretary is what she'd dreamed about: dressing real neat, walking with her legs close together, in that switchy way secretaries always had on TV, typing and filing and so forth. She must have been about ten years old when she'd hoped for that, not old enough to know that chubby-butt, black-skinned, unwed mothers with GED diplomas and short, nappy hair didn't get jobs as downtown secretaries or very much else, besides floor-moppers or whores, unless they had a college education. She'd had to drop out of school to take care of her son. She'd never considered marrying Carl's father and he had never asked if she wanted to get married. They were both fifteen and had only had sex twice. Since then, it seemed she only met two kinds of men—those she didn't like who liked her and those she liked who weren't interested in her. Her marriage dream was no more real than any of her other dreams. She lifted a slim, black pen from its desk holder, shined it on the edge of the apron she wore over her uniform and quickly replaced it.

But hadn't she at least suspected, even back when she was ten and still dreaming about secretarial school and happy-ever-after, that this was what her life was going to be—just what her mother's life had been and that of all her girlfriends who were not in jail or on dope or working themselves to death for some pimp or factory owner? Hadn't she known that questions like: "And what do you want to be when you grow up, little girl?" were only grown-ups' way of not talking to her, since they already knew the limits of her life?

A longing beyond words welled up from her core and threatened to escape into a moan so deep and so wrenching its gathering made her suddenly short of breath. She rose quickly from the chair and headed for the door.

What happened to the part of yourself that dreams and hopes, she wondered. Was it just a phase of growing up, to believe you might amount to something, might do something with your life besides have babies and be poor? And how come some people got to have their dreams come true and others didn't?

* * *

Lorisa lay with her head thrown back against the edge of the high steel tub, droplets from the swirling water gently splashing her face, tightening the skin across her forehead. She stopped by the spa for a whirlpool bath and fifteen minutes in the steam room every day after work. As a reward, she told herself, without thinking about what there was about her work that warranted rewarding. She shifted her weight, careful to keep her feet from the sucking pipe that pulled the water in and forced it out to knead and pummel her muscles, dissolving the tension across her shoulders. But not quite.

Jim Daily's face rose behind her eyelids—a pale, oval moon altering the landscape of her leisure with its sickly light. She pressed her eyelids down as hard as possible, but Daily's face remained.

"You notice how much she looks like the maid in that cleanser commercial? You know the one I mean," he'd gone on to whoever was in earshot, to whoever would listen, as he'd circled her, trapped her with his penetrating voice. "Go ahead," he told her, "Put your hand on your hip and say, 'Look, chile!' " He'd transformed his voice into a throaty falsetto. His pale blue gaze had pinned her to the spot where she stood, like a spotlight, as he'd waited for her to perform, to act like some nigger clown in some minstrel show. All in fun, of course; just joking, of course; no offense intended, of course. A hot flush of shame had warmed her cheeks. Is that how she looked to him, to them? she'd wondered, searching her mind for real similarities between herself and the commercial caricature of whom Daily spoke, even though she knew in her heart that he never saw her, that all black women's faces were most likely one to him.

Lorisa tried to let go of the memory, to give herself over to the soothing water, but her back was stiff now, her tongue pressed too firmly to the roof of her mouth behind tightly clenched teeth. All the rage she couldn't let herself release at the time came roiling to the surface in a flood of scenes in which she said all the things she might have said to him, if she'd had the luxury of saying and acting as she pleased—like the cleaning woman in her office. She saw herself putting her hand on her hip and telling Daily what an ignorant, racist dog he was. A stiletto-thin smile curved her lips at the thought of how he would have looked, standing there with his face gone purple and his whiny nasal voice finally silenced.

Of course, from Daily's point of view, from the firm's point of view, she would only have proved conclusively that all blacks were belligerent and had no sense of proportion, none of the civilizing ability to laugh at themselves. And, of course, she would have lost her job. Daily was slightly senior to her. He was also a white male in a white male firm where she, and the two white women consultants, did everything they could to distract attention from the fact that they were not biologically certified for the old boys' club. And Lorisa knew she was on even shakier ground than the white women on staff.

She was the one who got the smallest and most mundane clients with whom to work. It was her ideas that were always somehow attributed to someone else. She was invariably the last to know about changes in the firm's policies or procedures and office gossip was stone cold by the time she heard it. For a while, she'd been fairly successful at convincing herself all this was due to her being a very junior member of the staff, that race had nothing to do with it. Of course, she realized, with the seventh sense of a colored person in a white society, which members of the firm hated her silently and politely because of her color. Daily was not alone in his racism and he was probably less dangerous, with his overt ignorance, than the quiet haters. But they were individuals. The firm was different. The firm was only interested in making all the money it could. It didn't really care who did the work. Wasn't that what she'd been taught in her college economics courses? But more and more, as men with less seniority and skills than she were given serious responsibilities, she was increasingly unable to plaster over the cracks in the theory that the firm was somehow different from the individuals of which it is composed. More and more she was forced to accept the very good possibility that she'd been hired as a token and would be kept as a company pet, as long as she behaved herself . . . or until some other type of token/pet became more fashionable.

It seemed ironic that in college she'd been one of the black students most involved in trying to better race relations. She'd helped organize integrated retreats and participated in race work-shops. She'd done her personal share by rooming with a white girl who became her best friend, costing her what few black girlfriends she'd had on campus. She could almost count the number of dates she'd had on one hand. There were only a few black boys on campus to begin with and a third of them were more interested in her white roommate or light-skinned colored girls than they'd been in the likes of her. Those who had dated her had done so only once and spread the word that she was "lame," and "cold." She quickly evaded the thought that her love life hadn't improved appreciably since college. Back then, there were times when she had felt more comfortable with some of the white kids than she had with some of the black ones, although she'd denied this vehemently when a black girl accused her of it. And she'd originally liked being the only black at Carstairs and Carstairs. She'd thought she'd have more of a chance to get ahead on her own, without other blacks and their problems and claims to her allegiance.

"We're so proud of our Lorisa," her mother's prim school teacher's voice repeated inside Lorisa's head. The occasion had been a family dinner honoring Lorisa's completion of graduate school and the job offer from Carstairs. "Yes, indeed," her mother had gone on, "Lorisa is a fine example of what a young colored woman can do, if she just puts all this race and sex mess behind her and steps boldly, acts forcefully on her own behalf."

Lorisa wondered what her mother would say if she knew how often her daughter longed for just one pair of dark eyes in one brown face in which to see herself mirrored and know herself whole in moments when she was erased by her co-workers' assumptions about her ability or brains based on her color, not to mention her sex. It was only now that she, herself, realized how much she needed for that brown face to belong to a woman. How long had it been since she'd had one of those I-can-tell-you-cause-you're-just-like-me talks that she remembered from her late childhood and early teens? But that was before she and her girlfriends had been made to understand the ways in which they were destined to compete and to apprehend the generally accepted fact that women could not be trusted.

Still, she'd been smart to keep her mouth shut with Daily. The economy wasn't all that good and lots of companies were no longer interested in trying to incorporate blacks. She could have opened her mouth and ended up with nothing more than her pride. No job. No money. No future. She picked at the possibility like a worrisome scab, imagining herself unable to pay the rent on her newly furnished and decorated apartment or meet the payments on her new car, living a life of frozen fish sticks and cheap pantyhose in a roach-ridden apartment. She saw herself clerking in a supermarket or department store, waiting on people who had once waited on her. Or worse. The face of the cleaning woman from her office replaced Daily's in her mind's eye—the woman's scowl, her hands in cheap rubber gloves, her eyes showing something hot and unsettling, like the first glow of an eruption-bound volcano.

They said it wasn't like the old days. Nowadays, blacks could do anything whites could do. Hadn't a black man gone into space? Hadn't a black woman been named Miss America? Then why was it, she wondered, that the minute she began to contemplate being out of work and what would be available to her, it was only work near the bottom that she expected to find? It was as though her degrees, her experience and skills would amount to nothing, once she descended into the ranks of the black unemployed.

But she was not going to be unemployed. She was not going to be on the outside. She was from a family of achievers. Her father was the first black to get an engineering degree from his alma mater. Her mother had been named best teacher by the local parent-teacher's association for three years in a row. How could she ever explain getting fired to them? Or to members of the black business women's association she'd recently joined? No. She intended to stay right where she was and prove to Carstairs and Carstairs that she was just as dedicated to profit margins and sales, just as adept at sniffing out a rival's weakness and moving in for the kill, just as practiced in the fine art of kissing her superior's ass, as any white boy they could find. She rose quickly from the tub and snatched her towel off the rack, irritated that relaxation had once again eluded her.

*　*　*

The room was starting to have that acrid, funky odor of people in danger of losing their last dime. Jackie looked around the card table. Light bounced off Big Red's freckled forehead; his belly was a half-submerged beach ball bobbing above the table. Mabel's lips were pressed near to disappearance. It was a look she'd wear as long as there were cards on the table. Her gambling mask, she called it. Bernice was half drunk. Jackie hated playing cards with drunks. They either knocked over a drink and soaked the cards, or started some shit with one of the other players. Bernice had already signified to Alma about the whereabouts and doings of Alma's old man, Rickie, a good-looking Puerto Rican with a Jones for blue-black thighs. Ramrod Slim sat just like his name. His color and the millions of tiny wrinkles on his face reminded Jackie of raisins and prunes.

Jackie riveted her eyes and attention on Slim's hands as he passed out the cards. The hand he dealt her was as indifferent as all the other hands she'd been dealt tonight. Sweat formed a film separating her fingers from the cards. Oh Jesus! If she could just win a couple of hands, win just enough to pay on Carl's dental bill so the dentist would adjust the child's braces. She gritted her teeth at the memory of the note Carl had brought home when he went for his last visit, a note saying he shouldn't return without at least a fifty-dollar payment. Bastard! Honky bastard! All they ever cared about was money. But, of course, it was more than the dentist's money she needed now.

When she'd decided to get in the game, she'd told herself she had twelve dollars' card-playing money. If she lost it, she would leave the game and not have lost anything other than the little bit of extra money she had left over from her bills and other necessities. If she won, there'd be money for the dentist and the shoes she needed so badly. She'd found a quarter on the way to work—a sure sign of luck.

But not only had she lost her twelve dollars, she'd also lost her light bill money, all of her carfare for next week and was now in danger of losing part of her grocery money. She gripped her cards and plucked. Damn! Shit on top of shit. She wasn't hardly in the way of winning this hand. She longed for a drink to take away the taste of defeat, to drown the knowledge of once again having made the wrong decision, taken the wrong risk. She would have to get some money from somewhere. She let her mind run over her list of friends in order of the likelihood of their being able to lend her something and was further disheartened. Almost everybody she knew was either laid off or about to be. Those who were working steady were in debt and had kids to feed, too. She didn't have a man at the moment. The last one had borrowed twenty-five dollars from her and disappeared. But she would have to find the money somewhere, somehow. She wondered what it would be like to be able to lose this little bit of cash—not much more than a pair of those alligator pumps that woman had worn in the building where she'd cleaned yesterday. She tried to make space in her anxious mind in which to imagine having enough money not to constantly be concerned about it.

"Girl! Is you gonna play cards or daydream?" Big Red grumbled.

Jackie made a desultory play, waited for her inevitable loss, indifferent to whom the winner might be.

* * *

The Carstairs were consummate party givers. They liked entertaining. They liked the accolades providing lavish amounts of expensive food and drink brought them. It was what they did instead of donating to charity. Mr. Carstairs invariably invited all the professional members of the firm and made no secret of how much pleasure it gave him when they were all in attendance. As usual, on party nights, the front door of the Carstairs' twenty-room country place was wide open. A jumble of voices underscored the music that danced out to meet Lorisa as she walked slowly up the front steps.

She hoped it would be different this time. Perhaps, just this once, they would not all turn toward her when she first entered the room and leave her feeling blotted out by their blank, collective stare. She could have made it easier on herself by bringing a date, but she didn't know a man she disliked and trusted enough to subject to one of the Carstairs' parties, or a man who liked her well enough to make the sacrifice. Nevertheless, she attended all the Carstairs' parties, always leaving just as someone started banging out "Dixie" on the piano or telling the latest Jewish, Polish, or gay joke. She knew who would be the butt of the next go-round.

But tonight, she would do more than put in a respectful appearance. Tonight she would prove she was prepared to make whatever sacrifice necessary to play on the team. For she'd decided that it was her non-team player behavior—her inability to laugh at a good joke, no matter who was the butt of it; her momentary appearances at office social functions; her inability to make other staff accept that she was no different from them in any way that counted—that kept her from total acceptance into the firm. Tonight, she would break through the opaque bubble that seemed to keep her from being seen or heard, making her as murky to the whites on staff as they were to her.

After the usual genuflection before the Carstairs and the obligatory exchange of comments about how very glad they were she could come and how pleased she was to be there, Lorisa ordered a stiff drink from the barman and began to circulate with determination. She stopped at one small grouping after another, asking about wives and children, looking interested in golf scores, remaining noncommittal on the issues of busing and affirmative action until her tongue felt swollen, her lips parched and stretched beyond recovery. And still she pressed on: dancing with Bill Steele; laughing at Daily's tasteless joke about a crippled child; listening to Mrs. Carstairs reminisce about Annie Lee, the dear, dead, colored woman who had raised her, while her mama languished on a chaise lounge with a twenty-year-old migraine. And still she pressed on.

And she thought she made her point. She was sure she saw some of them, the ones who counted—the ones who watched the junior staff for signs of weakness or leadership—smile in her direction, nodding their heads as though dispensing a blessing when she caught their eye. Her success was clear in the gentle hug from Mrs. Carstairs, a sign of approval that all the women in the office had come to covet. It was this sense of having proved herself worthy that made her decide to speak to Jill Franklin.

She'd had no intention of trying to enlist anyone in the firm in her struggles with Daily. While she felt one or two of them—including Jill—might be sympathetic, none of them had ever attempted to intervene on her behalf or had even shown overt empathy for her. But the flush of acceptance made her feel as though she had a right to make requests of staff, just like any other member of the firm. She'd been talking to Jill and Ken Horton, whose offices bordered her own, about baseball, until Ken's wife dragged him away. For a few moments, both of the women were quiet. Lorisa gathered strength from the silence, then spoke.

"Listen, Jill, I need to ask you something. You've been working with Jim Daily for a while, now. And you seem to know him well, get along with him. Tell me, is there anything I can do to make him stop?"

"Stop what?" Jill's voice was full of innocent curiosity, her face bland as milk.

For the first time, since she'd arrived at the party, Lorisa looked someone directly in the eye. Jill's eyes had that same blue distance she saw in Daily's eyes.

"Stop . . ." she began, searching desperately for something safe to say to cover her error.

"Hey you two! This is a party, come out of that corner!" Somebody Lorisa didn't recognize grabbed Jill's hand and pulled her out to the patio where some people were dancing. Lorisa went in search of the Carstairs and made her good-nights.

* * *

Jackie spotted Mr. Gus as soon as she pushed open the door. He was where she'd expected him to be this time of evening: on his favorite stool near the far end of the bar, away from the juke box in the front of the long room, but not too close to the bathrooms at the back.

"Hey, Miz Pretty." Harold rubbed his grungy bar cloth in a circle and gave her a wink. Cissy and her old man, Juice (so called for his love of it), sat in a booth opposite the bar and stared past each other. Miz Hazel, who ran the newspaper stand, nursed a mug of beer and a half shot of something while she and Harold watched a baseball game on the portable TV at their end of the bar. Jackie was glad for the game. Talking to Mr. Gus would be easier than if the juke box was going. And she did have to talk to Mr. Gus. She'd tried all her girlfriends, her mother and even her hairdresser. Everyone was as broke as she was. Mr. Gus was her last hope. She stopped thinking about all the years she'd promised herself that no matter how broke she got, she wouldn't turn to this sly, old, brown coot.

She slid onto a stool three up from Mr. Gus and told Harold to bring her a vodka and orange juice. She glanced at Mr. Gus in the long mirror hanging behind the rows of bottles in front of her. He was looking at the newspaper lying on the bar beside his glass. He didn't lean over the paper, the way most people would. He sat with his back straight, his head slightly inclined, his folded hands resting on the edge of the bar in front of his drink. The white of his shirt glistened in the blue bar light. She had never seen him without shirt and tie, despite the fact that he wore a uniform at work, just like her.

"How you doin', Mr. Gus?"

He looked up as though surprised to find her there, as though he hadn't seen her from the moment she stepped in the door, as though he hadn't been waiting for her since she was a little girl. Mr. Gus was a neighborhood institution. Being a man who understood the economic realities of most black women's lives, he'd cultivated two generations of little girls and was working on a third generation. He took them for rides in his car, gave them candy—all on the up and up, of course. He would never touch a child. He got a portion of his pleasure from waiting, anticipating. Many of Jackie's little playmates had come to learn they could depend on their old friend, nice Mr. Gus, for treats in their adult lives, too. Only now the candy was cash and the price was higher than a "Thank you, Mr. Gus." But despite the fact that she made next-to-no salary and had a child to raise, Jackie had never come around. Until now. Mr. Gus smiled.

"Anything in the paper about that boy who got shot on Franklin Street, last night?" Jackie craned her neck in his direction, her eyes seeming to search the front page of the paper, her chest thrust forward, in her low-cut sweater. She skipped her behind over the barstools between them, still pretending to be intent upon the headlines. But she was mindful of the cat-with-cream smile on his face. It was a smile that made her sure he knew why she was there; that he had sensed, in that special way some men have, that she was vulnerable, could be run to ground like a wounded doe.

She hadn't meant to drink so much, but Mr. Gus was generous. And he was an excellent listener. There was something about his attitude, his stillness and sympathetic expression that allowed women to tell him things they often wouldn't reveal to their best friends. They told their men's secrets, what they had dreamed about the night before and anything else that was on their minds, as though injected with a truth-inducing drug. To many women, what was a little sex for badly needed cash, after this kind of intimacy? It was a line of thinking Mr. Gus encouraged.

And so, Jackie had rattled on about her lousy job and what her supervisor had said to her and how hard it was trying to raise a boy alone. Mr. Gus nodded and tsked, asked a question or two to prime the pump when she hesitated, ordered more drinks and waited for the beg, the plea. And, of course, the payback.

But in the end, Jackie couldn't do it. She told him how badly Carl needed his braces adjusted and what a fool she'd been to lose her carfare and light bill money in a card game. But when it came to asking him could he see his way clear to let her have seventy-five or even fifty dollars, the same hard glint in his eye that had put her off as a child made her hold her tongue. She did try to get him to say his lines—to ask why she sighed so forlornly, or what she meant when she said, in that frightened voice, that she didn't know what she was going to do. But Mr. Gus refused to play. He wanted the beg.

He'd been waiting for it for a long, long time.

They left the bar together. Jackie now a little rocky on her feet, Mr. Gus unwilling to lose when he was so very close. He took her up to his place for one last drink. The smell of old men's undershirts sobered her a bit.

"I sure hate to see you in such a bad way," he said as she sat at his kitchen table trying to adjust her breathing to the bad air.

"Course, you coulda had all I got." He poured another dollop of Seagrams in her jelly glass. Jackie quickly drank it down.

"I don't know why you always been so mean to me, Miz Jackie." He rose and walked to stand behind her chair, kneading her left shoulder with pudgy fingers that radiated damp heat, like a moist heat pad. She willed herself not to pull her shoulder away. He breathed like a cat purring.

"Why you so mean, Miz Jackie?" He spoke in a wheedling, whiny tone, as though he, not she, were on the beg.

"You know Mr. Gus ain't gon let you and little Carl go wanting. Don't you know that, now?" He crept closer to the back of her chair, still moving his fingers in damp slow circles.

"I got me a little piece of money, right here in the bedroom; and I want you to have it."

*　　*　　*

At first, Lorisa had considered it a sign of her growing esteem among her superiors that she was chosen to take Stanley Wider, of Wider Housewares, to dinner for a preliminary discussion about his signing a contract with the firm. She was so grateful for any indication of growing favor that it hadn't occurred to her to wonder why she, a junior member of the firm, with no real experience with prestigious clients, shoud be given this plum. The Wider account had the potential for being very big, very important to the career of whoever pulled him in. Now that dinner with Wider was nearly over, Lorisa understood why she'd been chosen.

Mr. Wider was what the women in the office called "a lunch man"—a client who turned into a sex fiend after dark and could, therefore, only be talked to over lunch. Looking at him, anyone would think he was a kindly, trustworthy genteel man—like

Walter Cronkite. Only his eyes and his words told the truth about him. She smiled up from her Peach Melba into his lean, clean-shaven face to find his eyes once again caressing her breasts. He smiled sheepishly, boyishly, when he realized he'd been caught. But his eyes remained cold and hard.

Ralph Wider was a serious pursuer of young corporate women on the rise. In the sixties, when women began pressuring for more room at the top, he'd been bitterly against the idea. But a chance encounter with an extremely ambitious female sales representative had shown him the benefits of affirmative action. In his analysis, women in business fell into two categories: those who were confident and competent enough to know they didn't need to take their panties down to do business; and those who could be convinced that in at least his case, a little sex would get them more business than a lot of facts. He didn't meet many black ones and the ones he met were always smart. He figured they had to be to get high enough to deal with him. But he had a fairly good record of convincing category-one women to slip down a notch. The challenge added spice to his business dealings.

"We're very excited about the possibility of working with your people," Lorisa began, trying once again to introduce the reason for their having dinner together. "We think we can . . ."

"You know, I've always admired black women. You all are so . . . so uninhibited." He stretched the last word out into an obscenity. "I bet you can be a very friendly young lady, when you want to be."

This man is important, not just to the firm, but to my career, Lorisa reminded herself before she spoke.

"I'm afraid I've never been particularly famous for my friendliness, Mr. Wider, but I am a first rate efficiency specialist and I've got some ideas about how to increase . . ."

He lifted his glass in a toast as she spoke. "To freedom" he said with a sly grin.

Twice more she tried to raise the subject of business. Each time he countered with another invitation to spend a weekend on his boat or take a ride in his plane, or have dinner with him in his hotel room the following night.

She knew what she should say to him. She'd practiced gently

and firmly explaining that she did not appreciate passes as a part of her work. But she'd never had occasion to use that speech, before. And this man had the power to greatly improve her position in the firm, simply by what he said about their evening together.

"Excuse me," she said between dessert and cognac. She could feel his eyes poking at her behind as she headed for the Ladies Room.

She wrapped wet paper towels around her neck, careful not to dampen her blouse and held her wrists under the cold water tap to calm herself. Tears quickened in her eyes at the sudden desire to tell some woman her woes; to explain about *him* being out there wait-ing for her and what ought she to do. Somebody deep inside urged her to go out there, pour a glass of ice water in his lap and run like hell — the same someone who'd urged her to talk to Daily as though he had a tail; the same someone who'd urged her to major in archeology instead of business and to stop smiling at white people, at least on weekends. But she was no fool. She wanted the Wider account and the prestige of getting it. She wanted her salary, her vacations, her car. She wanted to prove she was just as good as anybody else in the firm. At the moment, she just didn't know why she needed to prove it.

Lorisa dried her hands, checked her make-up and straightened her shoulders. She couldn't come apart now. She couldn't let them think she was incapable of handling any task the firm gave her. For all she knew, she was being tested. She brushed at her hair and willed that frightened look out of her eyes. I have a contract to get, she told herself as she opened the door.

She stared at his slim, distinguished figure as she crossed the room. So deceiving, she thought, like a bright shiny apple turned to maggotty mush on the inside. But if she could just get him to agree to look at the prospectus. He rose as she returned to her seat.

"I mean it, little lady," he said as he sat down, "I think you're really something special. I'm sure I can do business with you!" he added with a smile as his leg brushed hers beneath the table.

*   *   *

If there'd been any way for Lorisa to avoid getting on the elevator with Jackie, she'd have done so. If there'd been other people she'd have had no hesitation about getting on. Other people would have kept her from speaking, as she now feared she might. She didn't look at the woman as she entered the elevator, but she didn't need to. She remembered those eyes. The elevator doors hissed shut before her. The lobby button was already lit so she had only to stand there. She kept her eyes straight ahead and wondered if the elevator always moved this slowly or if the damned thing was going to stall, leaving them alone together for the rest of the night.

Jackie studied Lorisa's back and tried to get up the courage to say something. This was the first time she'd seen the woman since their encounter a couple of evenings ago. She still felt bad about how she'd responded. She wanted to apologize, maybe even change her luck by doing so.

"I'm real sorry for the way I acted the other day. Let me buy you a drink to make up for it," she practiced in her head, even though she didn't have enough money to buy herself a drink. She saw the two of them walking down the street to Libby's Place where she knew she could buy a round or two on credit. They would sit in a booth near the back. The juke box would be off, so the place would be quiet enough for talk. The woman would buy her a drink in return and they would talk about what they needed to talk about. Wasn't no black woman's life without something that needed talking about. But none of that was really going to happen. She could tell from the way the woman stood that she didn't want to be bothered.

As the elevator reached the lower floors, Lorisa reached in her pocket, pulled out her leather driving gloves and smoothed them on over long, slim fingers. She tried to keep her attention focused on what she was doing and away from her urge to somehow make herself acceptable to the woman standing behind her.

"Girl, you sure are evil!" she heard herself saying in a way that smacked of respect for the woman's willingness to give her economic betters hell. She saw them walking out of the building together. She would tell the woman her name and offer her a lift. Their talk in the car would be slow but easy. They might discover they liked one another.

But, of course, that whole scene was irrational. Why should she take a chance on being insulted again? Why should it make any difference to her whether this woman considered her somebody worth being pleasant to? She pressed her lips firmly together as the elevator finally slid to a stop. She stepped quickly forward and brisk-stepped her way to the outer door, trying to put as much distance between herself and the cleaning woman as possible, before she did something she would regret.

After all, it wasn't as though they had anything in common.

ROSIE AND ME

Sarah Schulman

ROSIE SHELDON IS FROM the southwest side of Chicago, which doesn't mean anything to most people, but in Chicago, it says it all. I'm from New York so I know how important where you're from is. We met there, in school, which makes sense because a New Yorker is as likely to go to college in Chicago as someone from the southwest side, if they go at all. Her father's name is Andreas and he's a janitor. Her mother, Annalise, reads *People* magazine and sews for Zaires, a big schlocky department store chain. Once Andreas drove me through the neighborhood past Marquette Park. "It's the last white park," he said in broken English.

Rumor has it that when Rosie first came to school she read her bible every night before going to sleep. Somewhere along the line she made friends with this Jewish guy named Robert Goldstein and through a miracle of transformation and recruitment, Rosie ended up in the Socialist Workers Party. I want you to understand the magnitude of this event. When she was in high school and a cheerleader, her all blond, all Lithuanian football team would play an all black school from the southside. Rosie and her Lith friends would chant, "We don't want no watermelon, we don't want no fried chicken." So, to suddenly call herself a Trotskyist and start hawking *The Militant* on the quadrangle of a very conservative university was really a significant change.

Well, the Socialist Workers Party, being the Socialist Workers Party, Robert decided that Rosie should infiltrate the feminist group on campus to win them over to socialist revolution. That's how I met Rosie. She came to one meeting and by the second she was busy organizing everything with those skills she picked up in the party and, I suspect, in her Lutheran church youth group. Soon she was hanging around with us, partially out of fascination and partially out of tenderness, hanging out and talking and having fun in a way she'd never seen among those who considered themselves part of the lower class of the master race.

Now, I'm just like everyone I grew up with, or if not exactly just like them, they at least know three other people who are similar to me. Rosie, however, being who she was, couldn't place me right away. I mean she had heard of the stereotypical Jewish, leftist, intellectual lesbian who fucked men and took drugs and had dark hair. But, she had never experienced my way of dealing in the world. Sometimes she was nice to me and sometimes she was cold to me and usually not very loving. She also wasn't emotionally dependable, but every once in a while when no one else was looking, we would get down and communicate. We had a lot to say to each other. Her cousins, for example, were literally Nazis, with uniforms and the whole rap, and I don't have too many cousins, if you know what I mean, so it wasn't an easy thing for us to try and build a friendship. We drank over it, danced around it, had acid trips on it.

She also had these absolutely loser boyfriends and I am not exaggerating. I mean, Rosie, for all her ability to stand you up and let you down, is really a beautiful woman and I'm not pulling a shiksa goddess trip either. She's smart too, but still her men were dogs. At the University of Chicago there weren't many women and it was easier to get a man than to get a C, so Rosie should have been able to take her pick. I remember one guy, Marty, who always looked like he was dead. You'd walk into her apartment at eight in the morning and he'd be sitting on the couch drinking a six-pack. You expected to see a hypodermic needle sticking out of his arm. One night I crashed out on that couch with my head by her bedroom door and after a few minutes I heard the bed creaking up and down, up and down, on and on, and I felt sorry for poor Rosie, hoping it didn't hurt her too much, having that dead boy pump away.

Well, she liked to be in cliques and she liked to be in the popular crowd. Still, after two years I realized that as far as I had come in my life, Rosie had come farther, only we weren't in the same place because she had a longer distance to travel.

On campus in 1979 there were two feminist groups, the lesbian one and the straight one. We were in the straight one even though I, at least, had made out with four of the other women and suspected that similar activity was going on behind closed doors. We also shared boyfriends. They were known as "The Women's Union Boys." Even today when I run into an old friend from that group we can find at least two men who we both fucked. Our problem with our lesbianism was the same problem most women have with their lesbianism, we couldn't keep ourselves from feeling it, only from validating it.

Eventually Rosie got a job in the same restaurant where I was working and after the place would close down there weren't many bars open to hang out in. We did find one afterhours place though, and started drinking. Nowadays, when I go out drinking I don't drink very much because the people I go with don't drink that much, or if they do, they get tired instead of adventurous. Rosie was different. When we got together we could always put it away and come alive, take off our shirts on Blackstone Avenue at three in the morning, jumping from car to car. So, one night we drank a lot of Jack Daniels, because when you're a waitress you always have cash and you want to treat yourself well since the job is so disgusting. We bought each other doubles and went outside in the wet, leafy spring early morning in Chicago and made out on someone's lawn and went home and took our clothes off and kissed and went to sleep.

Then I went away and she went away and we parted on pretty bad terms. I was mad that she wouldn't let me sleep in her bed anymore and I still don't know what she was mad about. I really didn't expect to see her again so I returned to New York and she went back to the southwest side, hearing about each other every now and then on the grapevine. You could say I gave up on her, but that turned out to be the way our friendship was maintained. I never count on her for anything, I never expect her to be there, but somehow she hangs around in my life. For five years now, she's been there, precariously, but there, nonetheless.

Once in a while, high or lonely, I would telephone and encourage her to move to New York. Then I got a letter that said she was coming. She had left her most recent man and gotten involved with a woman. It was a Jewish woman named Susan and Rosie was happy and in love and Susan reminded her of me. Well, I felt really proud. It was like she had seen a dress I was wearing and went out and bought the same one.

When she got here we sat around and talked and had a good time. I showed her the books I was reading and she told me about looking for Lithuanians in New York, bringing her double life nine hundred miles. Time passed, and one day she cut her hair all punky like everyone else in my neighborhood. Then she started taking classes in things like "The Frankfurt School." Her vocabulary suddenly included phrases such as "post-modern romanticism." She even took the obligatory course in Marxist Theory at The New School and of course had an affair with her professor. She also started scheduling every minute of her life. That's an immediate give-away that someone has just moved to New York. There's a million things to do, so they feel they have to do everything. It was all starting to get on my nerves.

"Okay Rosie, we are just going to eat dinner. We are not going to talk about Bauhaus or Canetti or Hannah Arendt."

Rosie was trying to sneak into the glitteratti. I told her it was the worst thing about New York, all those fake intellectuals running around putting people into categories and writing books about it. But she wouldn't pay attention. She needed to think that it was all wonderful and that she could be a part of it just by wearing the right clothes and using the right words.

Then the news came, Susan was on her way, from Paris no less, where she was studying socio-structural-something-or-other-ology. My chance to meet the girlfriend. I wanted to see her, to like her. I felt like part of the reason she was there in Rosie's bed was because of years of my hard work. And then, finally, one hot night, they walked through my door together, Rosie and her Jewish lesbian lover. I didn't like it at all.

This woman would not stop talking, as if life were one long cocktail party.

"I grabbed a cab down to the Kitchen, they'll be showing my video work in the fall, lunch at Magoo's with my dearest friend, he's a conceptual artist. Sociology, it's such a good area."

Susan had to leave at midnight to meet some friends at the Peppermint Lounge, or "the Pep" as Rosie had started calling it. That left Rosie and me looking at each other.

"Well, what do you think of her?"

"I'm sorry babe, but she's self-centered, boring and overbearing." Then I felt bad. Maybe my own shit was getting in the way. I wanted to encourage Rosie, give her support for being with a woman. So, feeling like a good sport, I called up Susan the next day and invited her out for a beer, just the two of us.

We sat in the bar, not knowing what to say. Susan broke the ice by coming directly to the point.

"Rosie says you and I are exactly alike. No offense, but I don't see anything at all in common between us."

Then we looked at each other. I saw her dark hair, she looked at mine. I examined her big features, she checked out mine. We observed each other gesticulate wildly and talk loudly. We both look and act Jewish.

"Hey, I have this friend you'll really like, she's Black too." Susan laughed, but I was too tired.

I never found out if Rosie heard about our discussion, but the next time we got together, smoked a joint and sat on a stoop in the West Village, she got sort of sad.

"I've been thinking about going to California."

"Great, go." I always tell people to go. "Look Rose, you're young now, soon you'll be old and it'll be a lot nicer to say 'When I was young I went to California' than to say you'd never been."

Rosie put her arm around me which she never does.

"Why do you love me?" She never says things like that.

"Uh well, I don't know what to say, I mean, I'm not prepared to answer that question."

"I'm asking because you talk too much when you're with me and I feel that you're not listening to me."

Well, you know, on the one hand I should have felt good that Rosie was finally acknowledging that we have a relationship in which we actually feel things about each other, but her approach wasn't too great, methodologically speaking. Maybe I do talk too much, but she's been my friend for five years, she should be used to it by now. Besides, I don't complain when she mumbles emotionally with her hands in her pockets, I just chalk it up to cultural differences. So I talk too much. If she'd just talk louder, I'd hear her.

Anyway, I got mad and went home and didn't hear from Rosie for a couple of months. She's not the kind to call you up and say that she loves you and wants to save the friendship, she just lets it go. After a while I missed sitting with her in Ukrainian restaurants eating potatoes. We're both really peasants and need a lot of potatoes. I cased one place, hoping to find her behind a stack of pirogies, but no sign. That afternoon I went up to her apartment on 13th street, under the pretense of picking up my copy of *People In Trouble*. Her roommate said she had gone to California with Jimmy, her professor from The New School. Oh well, that's Rosie. That's the story of Rosie and me.

FRIENDS AND FORTUNES

Linda Hogan

WHERE I LIVE, people do things outdoors. Out in the open air, they do what wealthier and more private people hide inside their homes. Young couples neck beside the broken lilac bushes or in old cars parked along the street. Women knead bread on their steps, and sometimes collapse in a fury of weeping on the sidewalk. Boys break windows in the broad daylight.

We are accustomed to displays, so when Mr. Wrenn across the street has the DT's in front of his house, conversations continue. *What will be, will be, and life goes on,* as my mother is fond of saying. The men who are at home go over to convince Mr. Wrenn that the frogs are not really there. If that tack fails, they kill off the frogs or snakes with imaginary machetes or guns. While they are destroying the terrors that crawl out of the mind, the rest of us talk. We visit while the men lift their arms and swing, aiming at the earth, saying there are no more alligators anywhere.

"Lovely day, isn't it?" someone says. "Did you hear the Beelah girl ran off with the gypsy fellow? The one with long fingernails?"

I lean against the tree on the other side of my mother, like we are holding up the dry elm. "She didn't have fingernails at all," I say. "She is a chewer. Everyone knows that. She even buys hot stuff to put on them to break her out of the habit." My mother jabs me with her elbow.

"Him. He's got long fingernails. He's fancy as a rooster up for the fair." It is Mrs. Bell speaking. She is wearing a pink cardigan buttoned only at the top and her stomach protrudes from the tri-angular opening.

Mr. Wrenn grows quiet and the men sit beside him on his small front porch, a slab of cement. This day it is my father who is sitting with him. Father has been sick with his heart and he looks pale. Even sick, he is better than a telephone or a newspaper. He's right in the action. He knows everything that happens in the neighbor-hood. When June Kim, the Korean woman who used to live next door, stabbed her enormous husband in his massive stomach, my father was the first to know. He, in fact, surveyed the damage before driving the large, balding man to the hospital. And he is the first man on the scene of any accident. When a Buick drove through Sylvia Smith's bedroom wall, my father was the first man there, catching Mrs. Smith in her nightgown, her pale chubby hands try-ing to cover up the rollers in her hair.

He was also the one to speak through the police megaphone to Mr. Douglas who held his wife and kids hostage with a machine gun. "Hey, Doug." My dad called him that for short, like he calls Mr. Smith by the name of Smitty. "Hey Doug," he yelled. "Don't make it any harder on yourself." And so on about how Marge Douglas wouldn't really leave him this time even though Mrs. Martinez had given her spells and charms to help her get away. "Doug. You are a logical man. You know you don't believe in any of that magic crap."

Women sat on the curb, their legs spread like crickets, their dresses great flowered hammocks pushed down between their open thighs. The police did little. They were only interested in how Mr. Douglas got a machine gun and the ammo. They don't really care who shoots each other out here. They don't even answer calls from our neighborhood at night.

I remember the women talking from the curb. "Maybe the crazy loon will shoot himself. I'm going to give Marge some of my gro-cery money to get away."

"Shoot. You know she won't ever leave that bastard."

"Watch your language. The kids'll hear you."

The women seem to know everything. They know why Mr. Wrenn drinks so much and they are pretty good to him. I like to be with the women. They know, for instance, when a man with a gun will really use it. They can feel it in the air. Maybe the direction of the wind or the vacuum heat of summer. They know Marge is more afraid to leave her husband now than she ever was, that she will instead find ways to get the kids away into early marriages, lives of being orderlies at the hospital, and then she will settle down to old age with Tom Douglas who will become slow and feeble and stupidly sweet. The women know, and have said, that Douglas will be one of those men who spend hours folding handkerchiefs into the shapes of birds and the shapes of women's pointed brassieres, hours tending the few eggplants that will grow in his small plot of garden and when no one even likes eggplant. Children will like him. The women know that. They also know that children will dislike the bitter and grumpy Marge when she is aged and wrinkled and full of anger from living beside Tom who will tell the same stories day and night as if she's never heard them, her scrubbing and sweeping, him story-telling about his wonderful life.

The wide-hipped women know just about everything, including how many books of green stamps it takes to get a bathroom scale or an electric mixer, and they talk about what they will get while my dad returns from Mr. Wrenn's.

But even with all their knowing, the people who are new to the block are still a mystery to the women. The Peñalba family moved into the house next door when June Kim and her husband moved out. The Peñalbas don't do much of their living outside. They seldom come out at all except when the mother and daughter go to church. Then the two females walk solemnly down the street in black old-fashioned looking dresses and black veils on their heads. They walk like a procession, the daughter trailing along behind the mother.

The daughter, Nora, is my age. She speaks with an accent and looks older than us Indian girls in the neighborhood. Her flesh has a gray light around it, like the grayness around the sick. Her house has the odor of burning. There is something feverish about it. Maybe it is the new shabbiness around it, or the way light hits some of the windows now that it is spring. The house is like the great eye of a tornado that all the crows have disappeared into.

*   *   *

The streets are brown in the morning light. All the tiny houses fit closely together in the early shadows. They are painted. Some are green, some pink or gold. Occasionally there is a dark brown house as if the tenant wished to make the house invisible, or like a house of the forest. I hear people singing sometimes in the bathrooms, or fighting in the kitchens. I like the sounds.

Last night it rained and now the streets have water rushing in the gutters, climbing the curbs. The water passes over some broken yellow dishes and old leaves that look lovely in the gutter, like something rich and exquisite, like gold in Venice in the history books. I stop to look. There is an earthworm drowning in the water and it is very thin and pale. I take it out and place it on a patch of earth.

Nora Peñalba is suddenly standing beside me, come as silently from the black hole of her house as the quiet air that surrounds it. She is not wearing black. She has changed into a brightly flowered, low-cut dress that makes her look much older and more knowing than anyone else in El Grande county.

Steam is rising off the street in the first sunlight and it surrounds her like fog around a new crop of tulips. Nora has very loose hips. When she walks, it is indecent the way her skirt swings from side to side, her thighs apart and natural, but I like the way she walks and I practice it alone in front of the mirror. She has black curly hair with red highlights. She is lovely, but whenever I look close I notice that grayness, and a secret.

Now she comes outside occasionally at night, but we seldom speak. We walk together to school. She goes with me because the tiny blonde social worker who wears expensive gray dresses has visited Mrs. Peñalba and told her that she is breaking the law if her children do not attend school. Mrs. Peñalba hunches over and looks at the floor. Nora translates between Señora Peñalba and Frau Betty, as my father calls her. To the tiny blonde with white nail polish and lipstick, Nora says things like, "Mama says we attend schools. We do not go against none of the legals." She has looked up the words in her dictionary in the presence of Frau Betty. She says such things as, "Yes, we are not citizens. We have been them a long while."

Her English is better than mine and I do not understand why

she cannot speak with the little blonde. I imagine it is because she is afraid of her, as we are all afraid of the people from the county. But Nora reads the newspapers, unlike the rest of us, although she does not bother much with school. She understands, though, when I talk about nothing but boys and how I am going to fix hair for a living when I am done with school. She understands my eyes following the two GI's that moved in down the street and that play loud music. She understands when I dress up and sit outside at night looking off in the direction of that house, but she is silent and holds an anger in her blood. "Like a spitfire," my mother says.

"I don't understand," Nora has told me, "why in the North of America you girls do not hold hands and walk the street together. I think we aren't friends."

"Oh yes, we are friends," I tell her, "We are the best of friends. But the people here don't like that kind of touching."

"No, then we are not friends."

Maybe we aren't. She is so burning and deep. Somewhere in my stomach I feel that we can never be close. And also, my mother does not like her. As Nora and I walk to school, I hear my mother's voice in the back of my mind. "She is sneaky, that girl," my mom says to Sylvia Smith across the street. But Sylvia changes the subject. Sylvia says, "I tell him I will even kiss his ass. In fact, I have done it." I listen and make a silent vow to never get married. I can see up Sylvia's skirt which is much too short for a woman her size, see her white ragged underpants.

"Besides," my mother says, "there is something wrong with them, something not right in their house." That's the way they talk, two distinct conversations.

"I would do anything for him. That man. And then he runs off and leaves me all week with his retarded son." Mikey. That is the son's name. And my mother, behind Sylvia's back, says Mikey is retarded because of the way they beat him, and beat him in full view of the neighborhood, right out in front of the house. I feel sorry for Mikey and for his sister, too. Their dad eats steak for supper when he is home and the kids must sit in the other room and have only a bowl of cereal. But Sylvia, herself, is a good woman who goes to confession to tell how poor a wife she is, and she does her penance.

"They put their garbage in the back yard," my mother says. "On the ground. And there are flies all over the place. The old woman doesn't even bother to brush the flies away from her face. She hardly moves at all. She just sits with the flies all around her."

"Yes," says Sylvia, shocked into my mother's conversation. "And almost all of their windows are broken and they don't seem to give a darn."

"And with all those flies," Mom says, and then changes her tune. "But that isn't their fault. The local boys asked for protection money and broke their windows to get it."

"Those damn boys. I wish they'd all fall into hell. Where do they get off terrorizing the neighborhood and making us pay them not to wreck our places?"

Today I have some money to see Mrs. Martinez about my future. I walk to her house, making notes in my mind of all I want to ask her. I want to ask her if I will be a beauty operator, if I will get a date with that tall boy in class, Mike Nava. I want to ask if I'll have children or go someplace exciting. There are small lizards near her house. I frighten them from the sun and they go into hiding beneath the foundation and under the shingles. Mrs. Martinez lets me in.

"Are you happy?" asks Mrs. Martinez. She is robust and wears long gold earrings.

I am surprised. I have seen her three times and she has never asked me about happiness. I have nothing to say. I haven't thought about whether I am happy or not. I had a conversation with Deborah, a girl who used to live a few blocks over. Deborah claimed to have once lived down a street from Marilyn Monroe. I remember saying to Debbie that all I wanted was a nice man and he didn't need to have money because that wasn't the key to happiness. Love was everything, I said. Deborah said she wanted the money and could toss away love because it never lasted anyway, like her mom and dad, for example. In fact, she said she had done away with love already because all the fellows from families around here would never amount to a hill of beans, let alone a house with a swimming pool or a big yard with white plaster statues of swans. She told me about a woman she once knew who even had the cloth for her bedspread imported from Germany, ancient and rich cloth. I didn't believe her. That was last year. I was younger. Then I never believed anyone lived much differently than we did. Now I look at the houses on television and I see what those people live like and it is better than here, even if they don't have much going on outside at all.

Mrs. Martinez heats water for the tea. While it is simmering, she takes out the cards and places them on the green card table where I am sitting. She prepares the tea leaves in the blue china cup. I look at her clean white stucco walls trimmed with enamel red and wonder if she got the money for the red paint from Mrs. Douglas who will never leave her husband.

I drink the tea and Mrs. Martinez looks into the leaves. She says that she sees a dog and a star. I am going to be a star in the world like that very bright one, the morning one, Venus, she says, shining early in the morning when the others have faded. She tells me I will live long, like that star. She asks me if I once had a dog that died. I did, but I don't ever give her too much information about my life because then she will be able to figure me out and my money will be wasted with her.

Mrs. Martinez doesn't even put her hand to her forehead when she says, "No, you won't date that tall boy. You will not have many dates at all because you are going to be following that star alone." Then it is time to look at my palm. It is upturned and a very lovely rich color. I like the lines on it. They are like fish nets cast out upon some river or sea. I have many lines and my palm is almost as cracked as my mom's geographic tongue. Mrs. Martinez touches each fissue and she tells me that I must be patient for three years and that I have a friend who will teach me all about life.

When Mrs. Martinez is finished, I give her two dollars. She looks deep into my eyes like she is reading my soul and she tells me, earnestly, that I have hope and I must find a way to get an education and must study hard at school.

I don't like the solemnity of it, but when I leave I feel lighter and happier. I can tell that my future is full of excitement. When I walk by the preacher's house I remember how I used to get saved every Friday just for something to do, go into the back room with the man and the other children and kneel at the bed and say I believed and beg forgiveness for my sinful thoughts. Now I feel as light and relieved as I did when I used to get saved.

At home, at night, I am sitting on the bed and staring at the gray tile floors. I am not happy. I wonder what has gone wrong with my life. I can think of no living reason on God's green earth for my despair. There is something greatly wrong in the world and something wrong in myself. But I do not know what it is. It's the first time I have thought about happiness and now I know that I have none. Damn Mrs. Martinez, I think, and then feel afraid that, all the way up the street, she will read my thoughts and curse me. I brush the words out of the air before me like they are stolen smoke from a cigarette.

I can hear my mother in her bedroom closing a drawer. I call her and she comes. My father is sitting in the living room in his favorite chair eating peanuts and I imagine his animal warmth and the smell of his shirt. But it is my mother I want.

"What is it?" she asks and I look up at her with my sad eyes. She is wearing her blue robe and a blue hairnet. "What is it? What's wrong?"

"Are you happy?" I ask.

"What kind of question is that?"

"I'm not a happy person."

"Nonsense, Sarah Bernhardt. Of course you are. What's there to be unhappy about?"

I can see that she has never thought about it either, and now it is an even deeper and more troublesome question to me. I wonder if anyone asks themselves if they are happy. Mrs. Martinez has probably ruined my entire life.

My mother says, "It is probably time for your period and so you feel blue." But when she leaves I look in the mirror and see, as if for the first time, my face. It is very pale although I am an Indian and I think perhaps that is what is wrong with me. My eyes are very dark and lonely and they are mysterious in a way I have never noticed, as if Nora's presence were haunting me from the inside out. I put orange lipstick on my hair to see if a tint or a rinse would make me happy but it doesn't look good. I wipe it out with a Kleenex. And then I lift back the covers of my small bed and crawl inside. I stay awake until long after the folks are in bed and I listen to them talking and do not feel comforted.

I think, this morning, that if I wear a yellow dress I will feel happy. As I put on my slip, I look out the window, pull the curtain back to check the weather. Nora and her mother are returning from early mass, dressed like funeral mourners, in black. Nora's younger brother follows them and he is wearing a white shirt. They look tragic and beautiful on the street, walking in the spring light, in the diffuse air that is charged with electric sparks of pollen. Nora's youth is hidden in the black cloth.

I dress and eat some toast and wear a rhinestone barrette in my hair. I leave the house early and go sit on the curb, careful not to dirty my daffodil-colored dress. Nora comes out early also, dressed in red. She sits beside me. It is too early for school but we sit in the sunlight like new flowers.

"Oh Nora," I say. "I am not happy."

She looks at me with her great nocturnal eyes, and says nothing.

"I don't even know when this sadness began."

"Maybe I'll tell you something happy. About the rain in Nicaragua."

"You're from Mexico?"

"No. It is more south than Mexico. And it rains. Warm rain. There are green and blue seas and rain forests of rosewood and balsa and cedar. With vines. In them live tiny, tiny monkeys and birds you call parrots with big eyebrows. It is like a paradise of the bible, the garden called Eden. In the night you hear the monkeys chattering about their boyfriends and the big cats roaring in the jungle out there like this, Grrr." She looks fierce. I lean back laughing. "Raar," she yells again, with her hands open like claws. "And sometimes the earth quakes to tell us we have been bad. It roars too."

I try to see it, but I don't. I feel badly that she is giving me some vision of her world and I can't form it in my mind. I wonder what shyness has kept me from asking her about her life.

"What color are the houses?" I ask her.

"They are, oh, they are house-colored." She laughs. It is a funny joke. And then she hisses, "Pah!" More a burst of air than a real word. "Of course you are unhappy, being so poor for North Americans." She gestured about in a wide circle and her hand's motion opened my eyes like a camera. For the first time I saw it, the two of us like bright flowers growing out of bulbs, blooming one time only before the winter, surrounded by the oil rags beside cars that did not run, beside the sea-green shards of Coca-Cola bottles that the boys had broken at night, and beer cans, the old yellowed newspapers stuck in fences and trees, saw a few children outside crying, two little boys hitting the earth with sticks that were also used as rifles for playing soldier. I do not think she means it, that we are poor. I think she is making fun of my unhappiness, and I want to be away from her. My body feels tense. I think of Linda at school who announces each week who she loves and I want to be with Linda, want to hear her tell me this week, as she does, "I am in love." I want to see the dreamy look on Linda's innocent face when she tells me she is in love with Rudolph Nureyev and I laugh at the foreign name and laugh even harder when she tells me he is a ballet dancer, laugh until she brings out the magazine picture of him all glorious and almost naked in that stretchy cloth you can see right through.

"It was Mrs. Martinez that caused it," I tell Nora. "When I went to have my fortune, she asked me if I was happy." Some hammering begins in the distance. It is rhythmic.

"I have tried to think when it first began." Nora is silent now and listening to me. "I think it began when the boys on the street were killing the lizards, were throwing them against the walls of houses and breaking them and the lizards would scream like people. And I know I am unhappy when Mr. Smith beats up his son, Mikey. And it all makes me sad." I feel about to cry.

Nora is quiet a long time and I know she is thinking of something. Then she says, "I think sometimes they are born bad. Men. I wonder too what makes them kill things. My own father, he was a good man and a leader of the people. He hated killings. There were so many killings the whole land was made of bullets and he always said we could rise up."

"What?" I think she is lying. A leader whose family is penniless and living right here in El Grande, next door to us?

"Yes. He was fighting against the government because they were cruel. You know, everywhere in the hot sun there were bodies.

My father wanted us to rise up. He got men together to battle the predators." She speaks so slowly now, and words I don't know and have never heard. I try to read the truth on her face. I don't know why she would lie to me. I am her friend.

"How do you speak of the deaths? They hung his head on a pole. When I saw it I began to scream but some old woman put her hand over my face and ran with me away from there."

I don't know how she can say such a thing. She is worse than our history teacher who has scared me half to death of the communists by telling how they will come and cut my brother in half in front of me and will make me choose between my mother and father and then kill them both. It all puts my nerves on edge.

"And they came and took my brothers. I adored my brothers. They were young." She is so matter of fact, as if she is saying nothing.

"Stop it." I put my hands over my ears. My face is burning. My dress is moist and my palms are wet. "Stop it. That's a lie. Shut your lying mouth." I stand up and I want to hit her with stones.

Nora stands up too. Breaking as her windows had broken. Her face is pale beneath her rouge and lipstick. She is in a rage, her entire body taut. "No," she screams. "It is true."

Something in her is falling away. It is also falling away in me. "It isn't true! It isn't. Let me alone!"

And she is hitting me in the face and grabbing my hair to pull it. I pull at her dress and we are twisting together on the curb, like flowers in a horrid wind. The people going to work around us are watching and pointing. She hits me again and again and I bend over to protect myself and then grab her to stop the blows while she breaks and screams. She stumbles away and falls, weeping, weeping all the rose colors of makeup over her chest. She falls and then she begins to run away while the children are shouting into the street and the gang of boys are cheering. I don't really hear them, just see Nora racing over the broken glass. Time stops. I have not believed and time stops. I have been pale and American, Gringa, as she calls me now, the screaming girl breaking as the windows of her house have broken, the girl who ran at me in a frenzy hitting me and me with nothing to do but hit her, to hold her and hit her back. As she runs away now, her fingers spread over her face, she is breathing in loud gasps and then she vanishes into the house, her footsteps gone and the door slamming behind her, and the wailing breaking the solitude of that house.

GOODBYE SUMMER

Tara Reed

"FUCK YOUR ASS to hell!" Kathy hung out the pickup window yelling at the three boys trying to cross the street in front of them.

"Calm down, would you?" Jill pleaded, turning down Washington to avoid the police station at the end of Government Way. "Get in here. You want anyone to see you out there and pull us over?"

"OK, OK, don't be so uptight." Kathy flopped back against the seat. "I just don't like it when people mess with me."

"You look pretty messed up already." Jill looked at her friend, tousled blond hair and black mascara circles under her eyes.

"Yep. I am." Kathy grinned. "I'm gonna get even messed upper if I can." She laughed and slapped the dashboard. "Messed upper alright."

Jill parked the truck in front of the long, low wooden apartment building they'd lived in since June. Kathy's face paled as the truck stopped. "Uh oh," she gulped, "I think I'm gonna get sick." She opened the door, leaned her head out and puked into the gutter.

As the sound and smell hit Jill she jumped out of the truck and ran up the walk, fighting her own wave of nausea. She unlocked the apartment door and yelled back, "Come on, Kathy, hurry up!"

Kathy stumbled up the walk, tripping on the door jamb. Jill caught her. She reeked of puke, scotch and cigarettes. "Shit, girl, you stink." Kathy slumped against the wall. "Oh, Christ, don't pass out now." Jill shook her awake and, half carrying her, threw her into bed. "Guess you'll have to wait till morning to get cleaned up," she said, pulling off Kathy's shoes. She left her asleep on the bed, fully dressed.

Crawling into her own bed across the room she glanced at the clock. One-thirty already and she had to be up by six. Well, she'd done with less sleep than that. She was getting real used to working all day tired.

*   *   *

Jill turned the battered, blue, three-quarter-ton pickup onto a little-used dirt road. She bounced up and down on the seat as dust flew up from her wheels. A few miles of this and she'd be down by the river. She pulled a cigarette from the pack on the dashboard. I've got to quit smoking, she thought, sticking it between her lips. She plucked the lighter from the coin pocket of her cutoffs and lit up, the taste of dry smoke mingling with dust. Jesus, it was hot today. Been hot for weeks. Dust covered everything, coating the dry yellow underbrush, turning the lower branches of the pines pale brown.

The road widened and ended at the river, a shallow green-blue furrow between banks of dry rock and pine. Nobody else was there. She and Kathy had discovered this place on a hot July day between their freshman and sophomore years in high school. Jill had just gotten her license and they were taking turns driving up and down the country roads in her dad's old blue Plymouth. Kathy had spun the car onto this old dirt road and there was the river, cold and blue, in front of them. She'd brought the car to a skidding stop, jumped out and threw off her clothes. "Hoo!" she'd yelled, "I believe we just found ourselves the perfect skinny-dipping spot!" They'd been coming ever since, rarely seeing anyone else. Now that they worked different times Jill came alone.

Most people cooled off in the lake where you could swim, float and lie around on beach blankets showing off your tan. Jill's tan started where her tee-shirt ended. She hadn't worn a bathing suit in years, felt barrel-chested and thick-thighed next to all those skinny girls. Even here, where she took off everything to swim, she never lay around naked afterwards. Her privacy was too tenuous. She didn't want to be caught by any boys from town out for a good time.

She parked the pickup off the road under a tree, hoping to keep the vinyl from getting too hot. Leaning against the front end, she watched the river and finished her cigarette. "Shit," she said, stubbing it out with the toe of her tennis shoe. The dust puffed up on either side of her foot, adding another layer to the already caked canvas. The car felt hot beneath her. Her stomach hurt with a dull, accustomed ache.

"I've got to talk to her," she said, scraping the heel of her left shoe down with her right toe and kicking the shoe off. She pulled off her tee-shirt and kicked off her right shoe. She paused for a moment, letting her breasts taste the sunlight. Then, stripping off her shorts, she ran into the river. The icy water hit her ankles with a bone-biting chill. She gave a loud whoop and dove into the middle, feeling the current sweep her downstream. Her feet scraped the bottom, found a boulder and held on. She stood, the cold water sweeping by her level with her breasts. Catching her breath, she gulped lungfuls of the hot, heavy air.

She dove back into the current, practicing her crawl. She'd read about some athlete who used to swim upstream a mile every day. She never swam very far but she loved the strong pull of her arms through the water and the strain of her legs kicking. It did seem like she could get farther upstream in a few strokes than she had earlier this summer.

She came out here almost every day after work, needing to swim the dust out of her skin and lungs. This was the second summer she'd worked as a flag girl for the highway. Last year she'd sworn she wouldn't be back. But the money was the best a girl could make around here unless she was slim and pretty like Kathy and old enough to waitress in the fancy cocktail lounges where the tourists flocked. This year Jill was old enough, but at 5'6", 180 pounds, with brown hair her mom called wavy and Jill called wild, nobody was knocking down her door offering her that kind of job.

She pulled herself out of the water, sitting for a moment on a rock beside the river to warm before pulling on her clothes. It was true Kathy made pretty good money, but between buying a few drinks after work at the bar and partying all day to "put herself in the mood" she was hardly saving enough to pay her half of the rent. Jill pulled on her tee-shirt. Kathy's being out of it all the time was giving her déjà vu of living at home with her dad.

She got up quickly to escape that thought. Slipping on her shorts, she retrieved her cigarettes from the truck. She sat back down by the river and lit up, allowing her naked feet to dangle in the cold stream. "Gotta quit these," she mumbled, inhaling. Maybe in the fall, after she'd figured out what to do next, she could calm down enough to quit.

She didn't even want to think about the fall. Maybe she could just get a job in town for the winter, save some money and postpone any decisions. Maybe she'd take a few night classes at the JC, keep her options open in case she decided to go to college after all. There were lots of two-year programs that would get her a good job when she got out. She sure as hell wasn't spending the rest of her life on a road crew.

She lay back, flinching at the heat of the rock against her skin. Thinking of school took her back to graduation night. She and Kathy had both turned eighteen during the year, so they were assigned to bring the booze. They'd sat in the pickup her brother Dan had lent her when he left for boot camp. Kathy had toasted Jill with the whiskey bottle, "Here's to the future, buddy. From now on we're working women!" It wasn't like they hadn't been before, Jill thought, but she'd known what Kathy meant: They'd be fulltime financially responsible women. The whole world had seemed to spread before her. They'd gotten drunk together that night, laughing and having a good time, planning what great things they'd be free to do.

Jill sat up. "Some great things," she snorted. She still worked road crew days and watched TV every night. The only thing different was she lived with Kathy now instead of her folks, and some difference that was turning out to be.

It seemed like all her life she'd been worried about drinking, first her dad's, then Dan's, and now Kathy's. She'd thought it was just that she'd always been a little scared of booze. Whenever someone got drunk she saw her father's face on theirs, that vacant, I'll-hit-you-as-soon-as-hug-you look that she knew so well. Lots of her friends got drunk sometimes. She'd even gone herself to the keggers out on Beacon Point. But Kathy was drinking almost all the time.

She picked up a small round rock from the water's edge. She rolled it between her fingers, feeling its smoothness. The velvety dust came off. The oil in her hands rubbed a shine into the grey stone. She tossed it into the river. The water erupted in a splash, then it was gone, even the ripples swept away by the current.

Jill stubbed out her cigarette and stuck the warm butt in her pocket to throw away later. She suddenly remembered a day just before her twelfth birthday. She had been sitting at the kitchen table while her mom cut potatoes into a stew for dinner. The late afternoon sun shone in golden patches on the kitchen counter. Outside the leaves were just beginning to turn. Jill peeked up from her math book occasionally, furtive glances taking in her mom's quick hands and the purple bruise under her left eye. "Why does Dad do that?" she had finally asked, her voice small in the bright room.

Her mother had looked at her tiredly. "It's the drinking that does it, he can't help himself when he drinks. You watch yourself, Jill. Stay away from drinking men. They don't know what they're doing and they're bound to hurt you." Then she'd gone back to peeling potatoes, the tilt of her head showing that the subject was now closed.

Jill picked up another rock and threw it. "It's not the drink that does it," she told the river. "It's his fist hitting her. That's his hand tipping the bottle. He's a bastard. Booze's just the way he shows it." She threw in a handful, the splashes hitting the water like a series of tiny bombs.

Retrieving her tennis shoes, she jumped into the pickup, spun it in a circle and headed back toward town.

*   *   *

When Kathy got home that night Jill was sprawled out in front of the TV. "Hiya," she said, flopping down on the couch beside her. "How's the road business?"

"Shitty as usual." Jill frowned.

"Oh oh, aren't we grumpy tonight." Kathy leaned back into the couch and picked up the TV guide. "Well, in case you want to know, the tourist-fleecing business is going just great. I got a twenty-dollar tip from some businessman type. He also left his motel key which I dropped in the mail slot on the way home. Jesus, what does he think I am?" She kicked off her three-inch heels, pulling her right foot into her lap for a massage. "Holy Shit my feet hurt! I was doing all right until Tina flaked out. She got sick again in the middle of her shift and left me with a double load." Reaching her long fingers into Jill's shirt pocket she pulled a cigarette from the pack stowed there. Lighting it with a lighter from the same pocket she continued, "I think she's pregnant." She inhaled deeply, savoring the smoke in her lungs. Curving her mouth and snapping her jaw she let out a smoke ring which she then swept away in a stream of smoke.

"Hey, Kathy," Jill forced out. Kathy looked at her, suddenly wary. "Did you stop for a drink on the way home?"

"I had a few with Jerry while we closed. Why?"

Jill inhaled slowly, afraid, then let it all out in a rush. "I'm worried about you, Kathy. I think you drink too much."

The words hung between them. Jill watched Kathy, barely breathing. She could hardly remember a time when they hadn't been best friends. Ever since Kathy's folks had moved to town in the second grade they'd been Mutt and Jeff. Now Kathy's red painted mouth cut a grim line across her narrow jaw. Finally, Kathy spoke.

"You're just spooked because of your dad. I know how you feel, my mom's no lightweight drinker herself. But I don't drink any more than anyone else you know. Look at Ann and Mary Jo, they party as much as I do. It just looks like alot to you cause you don't drink much at all." Kathy switched the channel on the TV. "Let's see what old Tom Snyder has to say tonight." She mimicked in a nasal voice, "My guest tonight is the world renowned Choco Cake-face, world famous cupcake eater."

"Cut it out, Kathy, I'm serious."

Kathy stopped clowning and turned to face Jill. "Drop it, OK? You don't know what you're talking about."

"What do you mean I don't know what I'm talking about?" Jill could feel her anger rising, a hot wave from her belly. Even as she said them, a part of her tried to pull the words back. "I'm a fucking expert I am. If I don't know a drunk who does? Seems like all I ever see are shit-faced, puking drunks. Well, I'm sick of it!" She jumped up, kicking over a footstool, scattering the full ashtray onto the floor. "I'm sick of you all!" she screamed.

Kathy sat for a moment in shock. Then she stood and walked out of the room.

"Where the fuck do you think you're going?" Jill yelled after her.

Kathy turned in the doorway. "If I'm gonna get called a drunk I might as well be drunk." She emerged from the kitchen a minute later carrying a bottle of Wild Turkey and a glass. "Want some?" She sauntered over to the couch and sat down. She shot back a bolt of the whiskey and poured herself another. She looked up and saw Jill staring at her. "What's the matter? Haven't you ever seen a shit-faced, puking drunk before?"

"Kathy, I didn't mean to . . ."

"Shut up!" Now Kathy's face flushed with anger. "You're just so high and mighty!" She spat out the words. "I don't care what you meant. If you're so sick of me then why don't you move out? I don't need some tight-assed bitch moping around me."

"Kathy . . ."

"Don't 'Kathy' me, just get out of here."

Jill turned slowly, walking into the bedroom they shared. "I'm not your fucking father!" Kathy yelled after her. Jill just shut the door.

The next morning Kathy's bed hadn't been slept in. Jill lay on her back for a long time, watching the dust dance in a shaft of sunlight from the window high on the wall. The air seemed thick, her body heavy. Images of her dad or Kathy passed out, vomiting and stumbling down the street alternated with memories of herself making coffee for them, cleaning them up, even lying for them. I'm tired, she thought, tired of helping other people fuck up.

She dressed slowly, glad it was Saturday. Her muscles felt strained and sore as if the fight last night had been with fists instead of words. As she entered the kitchen she saw out of the corner of her eye Kathy awake, curled on the couch drinking coffee. She looked up sheepishly. "Hi Jill, I'm sorry about last night. You know how I get sometimes, blow up at nothing and spout off my mouth.

Still friends?" ·

"Sure." Jill sat down beside her. On the TV screen a dog lit a dynamite cigar which blew his face off. "I'm moving out as soon as I can find a place." Jill stared at the screen as she spoke, her voice a monotone.

Kathy's face contorted. "Great," she exploded, "that's just great. And how am I supposed to make the rent alone?"

Jill continued to stare at the TV, unwilling to meet Kathy's eyes. "Tina's gonna need a place as soon as her folks find out she's pregnant. If she doesn't move in I'll wait till you find someone else."

"Oh great. So I get to play nursemaid to some knocked-up hippie. I thought we were friends, Jill."

Jill stood, shoving her hands in her pockets. "We'll be better friends when I don't live here." She shrugged. "You want some breakfast? I got eggs yesterday on the way home and there's bread for toast."

"What do you mean, 'better friends'? Sounds like a kiss-off line to me. So I had a few drinks last night. So what? It's not like you've never been drunk yourself. Come on, Jill. What's with you today?" Kathy got up and followed Jill, who had gone into the kitchen. She leaned against the doorway, watching Jill crack eggs into a bowl to scramble. Her voice softened. "Did something happen yesterday? Something with your dad?"

Jill just shook her head and poured the eggs into a pan. She took two pieces of bread from the bright red plastic wrapper and plopped them in the toaster.

"I don't get you," Kathy continued. "First you're yelling at me for drinking and then this morning it's move out and the silent treatment. Shit, Jill, I thought you were my friend, my best friend."

Jill looked up from stirring the eggs. "Kathy, I love you." The words caught in her throat. "But I can't take being around you when you're drinking all the time. It's not doing either of us any good. Now do you want some of these eggs or not?"

"No, I don't want any eggs." Kathy stood with her hands on her hips, blocking the doorway. "What I want this morning is a friend. But since there don't seem to be any of those around here I guess I'll just have to go somewhere else." She spun and headed toward the door. As she opened it she shouted back, "Don't bother waiting around to move, The sooner you're out the better!" The door slammed behind her.

Jill stared down at her pan full of eggs. A tight knot sat in her stomach. She scraped the eggs onto a plate, covered it with aluminum foil and put it in the refrigerator. Her hand shook as she poured herself coffee. "Shit!" she yelled and threw the cup against the far wall. It hit with a dull thud, denting the sheetrock. Coffee flew all over, splattering the floor, ceiling and walls. Jill sat down, leaning against the stove. "Shit," she whispered, tears spilling hot on her cheeks.

COMMON GROUND

Celia Smith

THEY'VE DECIDED ON Larry's Diner for old time's sake. Elenor arrives first and pulls out a paperback. It disturbs her to be in old haunts alone. She's been back in Allentown since the divorce two months ago, but has avoided familiar places, especially restaurants. Being a waitress has spoiled the pleasure of eating out. In a few months she'll have money to move somewhere interesting, Santa Fe maybe, though now that Iris is back she might stay longer. Since their reunion, the town has been less forbidding.

Iris said she'd be coming straight from the hospital, which might have been to warn her, Elenor thinks, about last minute emergencies. But then she sees her pushing through the door—in a white lab jacket, a beeper attached to her belt—and realizes the warning was about appearances.

Heads turn from the counter to watch them hug. "You really class up the place," Elenor jokes as they slide into the booth. She eyes the stethoscope looped like a pet snake around Iris's neck, but her friend seems briskly unaware of it. "I'm sorry, Elly," she says, "but I'm working with slave drivers this month. Only have half an hour."

"Hardly enough time to soak up the ambience." She chances a first look around; with Iris here she can invite the familiar, allow it to call forth connections.

"I know. The place has kept its uncompromising dedication to drear, all right."

They point in turn to the counter stool still missing its top, the old coat rack balanced by a pot cover, the string of tinsel hanging from the clock. They search for the peace sign Elenor carved into the wall eight years ago.

Then Stella appears, the same sluggish old woman who waited on them in high school. She gives them no sign of recognition. When she transfers coffee cups and a basket of saltines to their table, Elenor can feel the shifting balance, right below her stomach and along both arms. She remembers a night they ridiculed the deliberate, matronly care Stella took in setting their sundaes down.

"I can't believe she's still here," Iris whispers. "The same cannonball express."

Elenor feels guilty laughing. She glances towards the counter for a safer focus—there is Benjamin, one of Allentown's more respectable drunks, sitting across from the pies and cole slaw. Iris follows her gaze.

"Well, if it isn't old what's-his-name. Isn't he the one who got you fired from the Brewhaus?"

Benjamin had been at the alley door the night she got caught giving away stale kaiser rolls. "He'd just come by as usual," Elenor says. "I'm surprised you remember that."

"Remember? I about died from envy. I'm in New York, holed up with skeletons and diagrams— and you got your own Salvation Army going."

"Hardly that. It just made sense, that's all. Besides, I got fired and you got a degree."

She knows that will get Iris going. Their approval of each other has always come across in mock accusations that have to be denied. Only now Elenor isn't sure that either one of them feels approving.

"Some degree! Ups my status as a flunky, that's all. I know what they mean by 'intern' now, they never let me leave the place."

Elenor nods appreciatively through stories of round-the-clock shifts at Allentown General, surgery mix-ups and cafeteria chili. But her eyes keep returning to the pocket of the white jacket. Right below the pens and prescription pad, lined neatly along the top edge, is that small rectangular pin. It brings home to her what escaped in the exchange of letters and even the times they've seen each other up till now. This is the first time she's seen it in print: Iris

Keller, M.D. She supposes she should say something about it. She shouldn't have waited so long. The cool vinyl of the booth feels like a hand on the back of her neck, pushing her.

"I still can't believe you're a doctor." She shakes her head, uncertain about her tone of voice—was it complimentary enough?

"You and me both—what with three other docs checking my every move. They're afraid to leave me alone with a patient."

Elenor begins to relax. The white jacket is easier to accept with her old friend complaining in it. Iris's next reproach is aimed at a patient.

"He's there for a heart attack and sneaks his secretary in for dictation. Sees me and says, 'Can you come back later nurse?' It still blows their minds that not every woman in the hospital is a nurse."

Elenor has her elbows on the table by then. She's struck by a resemblance between their jobs.

"I just had a customer who reminds me of that guy. He brought his secretary to lunch and had her scribbling on a pad the whole way through it. I swear, those executive types . . ." She shrugs, pleased to have made the connection.

Then Iris gives her a puzzled look, and she realizes the stories don't compare after all, that Iris expected a show of indignation. But she's caught up now, determined to find common ground.

So they trade off. If Iris has a talkative patient Elenor has a lonely customer with bad breath. If Iris's attending physician is too critical, the restaurant manager won't allow Elenor ten minutes to sit down.

After a while, she notices a strained, restless look about Iris's face, and realizes her offerings are falling flat, as if there were insults hidden within them. Iris gives her a cautious smile.

"Have you thought of going back to school?"

Yes, of course she would want to know that. "Sure I have," she says, "off and on. But it's not like I have a career in mind."

She would wave the subject away if she could think quickly enough. Instead she becomes aware of Benjamin muttering to himself, watches Stella tip the coffee pot over his cup.

"But you're so great with people, Elly. You'd make a good counselor, or organizer or something. I bet you'd be great at social work."

Elenor smiles. "Have you been talking to my mother?" And suddenly she remembers Jim and the night she came home reeling from the Brewhaus and he told her to become a goddamned social worker if she wanted to help bums.

"Sorry," she hears Iris say, "I really don't mean to come on strong, but when you complain about your job. . . ."

Why is it acceptable for Iris to gripe but not her? She thinks of arguing the point, but submits to a suggestion that she has no point, a cool voice sighing—They don't make pins that say Elenor Hadley, Waitress, you dimwit.

Then Iris gives her that cheer-up look which horrifies Elenor, for she knows it covers embarrassment; she had meant to sound indifferent, even scornful, not dejected.

"Don't forget that I've envied you these years," Iris says. "Taking off on the spur of the moment, you and Jim, off to Colorado, off to California. Having adventures while I was stuck with *Gray's Anatomy*."

Elenor begins to feel like the grasshopper begging before the pragmatic ant. Her eyes are fixed on the stethoscope, which does *not* look like a pet snake; she imagines listening with grave competence to a heartbeat and feels chastised.

She has nothing, after all, to compete with being a doctor. Dreams, yes. But they're hardly translatable, these visions of reading Tolstoy and Jung, studying Greek mythology, learning wilderness survival. Some of them have evaporated with time—she and Jim discovered there were no jobs in the wilderness—and some she still clings to. She usually falls asleep with a book in her lap. Strongest of all is the idea of what she does not want—and to this she's stayed faithful, rejecting college, "respectable" clothes, and Jim too, when he kept pushing for "some stability." Stability meant children, which to her means being trapped. So how could she explain any of this to Iris, when none of it amounts to anything concrete and definite?

It's almost time to get away and recoup. Elenor talks too brightly about a night she'd played guitar in a roadhouse outside of Denver, exaggerating the few dollars in tips, making it sound like a job she had for weeks.

"See what I mean?" Iris encourages. "There's plenty you can

do. I didn't even know you were still playing. I'd love to hear your latest songs."

Elenor slouches in an armchair by the front room window, a book face-down in her lap. The book is a belated divorce present from Iris. YOU ARE THE BOSS roars up at her from one side of the glossy jacket; below it, in milder lettering: *A Guide for Redesigning Your Life and Career.* The author's jovial face fills the other side of the jacket. She stares at his mustache and balding head as if framing a rebuke, then imagines telling her mother she's decided to become a goddamned social worker after all. Her family would greet the news with triumph; they would say it was only that truck driver husband of hers holding her back all these years.

That is probably what Iris would say too, given the room. And Elenor has given her the room already, hasn't she, accepting that book like a penitent traitor: "Maybe it will give me a few ideas."

She lays the book on top of the orange crate by her chair. A couple of pens fall through the slats and land softly on the magazines below. If she leans out the window at a certain angle she can make out the clock in the bus terminal across the street. The 6:15 to St. Louis is just pulling in. By the time the loudspeaker belches, "Hamburg, Newburg, Harrisburg, Pittsburgh and all points West," she'll be leaving for work.

The ironing board clatters into position and she slips a gingham dress over the narrow end. Not enough time for a thorough job; she can never get close to those puffed sleeves without creasing them worse. While the iron heats, she leans against a window ledge to appraise her apartment. The circus poster she wrested from Jim, childishly displayed, buckling around its thumbtacks. The black guitar case lying like a coffin beside her mattress—she hasn't opened it for a year. The faded Indian bedspread that once signified a break from her parents, the bobbing leaves of the new mobile that just last month symbolized the break from Jim—they have all become clichés, and tonight when she gets home from work, she'll think about rearranging the place.

Elenor's latest job is at fancy new Mr. Bojangles on Hamilton Street. For three weeks she's made guarded and dismal conversation with the other waitresses while they wait for customers. But tonight she is glad to see them, even grateful for the piped-in banjo music they all hate. The whole crew is like family tonight. Brenda and Nadine, Charles the cook, the busboy Ricky. They would certainly get a kick out of that book. She wishes she'd brought it along to hear Charles snort, "YOU ARE THE BOSS? You bet your ass I am," that's what he'd say.

She takes a place by the table where Nadine and Brenda are folding brown linen napkins to look like two-pointed crowns. Their gossip warms her. It would never occur to them to apologize for being waitresses. She watches them as an apprentice would, as if there is a secret art in the way Brenda's red fingernails glide along the crease of a napkin. She's often studied them and suspects they see it in her, this trying to glean something beyond their practiced movements. She also knows they resent her for it, seeing the judgement there. For of course she does judge them; what she is admiring in Nadine's new hairdo is the perfect assurance she shows it off with, not the stiffly sprayed black coils that remind her of certain girls in high school. "Typing majors," Iris once dubbed them.

Now Elenor wants to be drawn in. She looks for an opening in their conversation, but is soon lost as usual in the twisting plots of soap operas and has nothing to say when the talk turns to children or microwave recipes. She drifts out the back door, stopping first at the kitchen garbage pail to lift out a few scraps.

"When you gonna stop feeding every damned alley cat in this city!" Charles yells to her back. "Don't you know they got diseases?"

Before she can answer, Nadine sticks her head into the kitchen. "Some friends of yours out there. Could you move them into your station?"

In the large dining room only two tables are occupied. Elenor sees Iris at once, smoothing a napkin over her lap. She's smiling at the man beside her; they're both wearing white jackets, which annoys Elenor: Doesn't she ever take that thing off? Ricky has just filled their water glasses when she approaches with menus.

"I've been meaning to surprise you every night this week," says Iris. She introduces David, "A fellow resident. We're doing OB together." Elenor waits with the stiff-backed menus resting against her arm like schoolbooks while David unfolds his napkin. The peaks of the linen pop up and separate—she's glad they hadn't seen her folding those things. David looks like a soap opera doctor, stiffly handsome and amused. She turns her head to see Nadine and Brenda watching from the coffee station. In the meantime she hears herself being introduced. As Elenor, "my old friend from high school."

"No," she tells herself walking away, "Oh no. Iris did not mean it that way. She meant 'my good friend *since* high school.' " It is beneath her to scrutinize words like that—if she doesn't stop she'll be hearing everything as a slight.

"I didn't know they were friends of yours till I already seated them," Nadine complains. "I thought you would switch them to your own station."

"Well I don't see how I can right now," she blurts back. "High and mighty doctors aren't used to being asked to move. I'll split the tip with you, if they leave one."

She is too angry to regret the words. If Iris is here to observe her old pal from high school as a serving girl, perhaps she should play up to it—on her way back towards their table she considers the effect of dropping into an exaggerated curtsey. She doesn't. Instead she hears her voice, deceptively shrill, recommending the Catfish Creole. A few strands of hair escape the barrette to fall forward over her eyes, and perspiration gathers under the puffy sleeves.

Back in the kitchen she comes up behind Nadine and Brenda in time to catch, " . . . like to hear her talk about her *enemies*."

It serves her right. Nobody trusts the one in the middle, the one without alliances. You have to take a side and stay put; it doesn't work to skitter back and forth trying to appease everyone. She lectures herself with these words, but calmly, reasonably, in order to keep from crying. Meanwhile Nadine lines three platters along one arm and with her other hand picks up a Crab Louie. She asks Elenor to follow with two baskets of cornbread; nothing in her voice suggests malice or discomfort, and her face remains seamlessly pleasant, as if the platters weigh nothing and she has just been chatting about a T.V. movie.

Elenor is entranced. Trailing Nadine with the baskets she feels like an apprentice again, but with some glimmer of the skill she must learn—that deft, bland, impermeable cover which the lacquered nails and sprayed hair only reinforce. The ability to remain untouched, to step through judgement as through an automatic door, without slowing down. It will take some time to perfect the skill but even now she can look over at Iris and David and see past the humiliation to just two people, customers, eating dinner.

"I wish you could sit here and join us for a while," says Iris.

"I'd like to but the manager should be walking in any minute. We're supposed to stay busy."

Elenor stays busy; ketchup bottles and sugar bowls need refilling, the tops of salt shakers should be polished. She is more than usually attentive to the three men at her other table, regulars from the Allentown Chess Club. They invite her to observe their upcoming tournament in the Sheraton ballroom.

She makes conversation with Iris and David at short intervals; they tell her about a staged disaster scheduled for the hospital next week—an accident at the steel plant, hundreds of casualties. She spaces questions between trips to their table—how are the victims chosen? Do they use props like fake blood?—all the while clearing plates or standing by with the coffee pot should another table signal.

She's run out of questions by the end of their meal, but at least they can't stay for dessert; they're late already, Iris says. They thank her as if she made the dinner herself. David hands her a VISA card and she totals the bill without leaving space for a tip. But she knows there will be one. As Iris is promising to call her soon she thinks of the tip smoothed out someplace on the tablecloth.

And when she finds it, after she's slipped it into her apron pocket, there will be one more embarrassment to get through. She must approach Nadine with half the money, as she said she would, and Nadine will tell her, pleasantly, to keep it.

ONE OF THEM

Valerie Miner

"THEY'VE TAKEN OVER Women's Studies," said the History Professor.

"They certainly make my wedding ring feel heavy," said the Associate Dean of Students.

"Always acting 'more feminist than thou,' " said the Poet-In-Residence.

Cornelia regarded her friends and realized this was a party of well-known feminists. Scholars who had taken risks for their politics. Some who always had a "gut feeling" for feminism. Women who had found Charlotte Perkins Gilman. Who wrote books about the tyranny of motherhood. And all of them "struggling" on the home front, too, with their bullheaded men. Almost all of them.

Naturally the conversation turned to lesbians. Cornelia knew why. The woman wearing the fedora had walked out into the garden. Cornelia listened to their complaints and imagined the garden as some sort of wild game refuge.

"They judge your feminism on your bed partner," said Barbara.

"Who does that?" asked Cornelia.

"Andrea Dworkin," interrupted Rose angrily, "says heterosexual sex is murder."

"It's their attitude that bothers me," shot Kim. "Like the aggressiveness of their clothes."

Cornelia knew these women well. Knew they appreciated irony. Self-irony. "There's a uniform?" she smiled.

Barbara looked past her, responding to Kim. "And the almost bragging display of affection." She stabbed a strawberry and grape together with her toothpick.

"I heard of a woman at Smith," whispered Rose, "who slept her way to the top of her department and it didn't have anything to do with phallic power."

"So lesbians are running the American university system?" asked Cornelia, still betting on humor. She tried to ignore the migraine starting behind her left eye.

Mariette considered Cornelia cautiously, obviously worrying her friend would do something rash. Even breathing too deeply in your year of tenure could be rash.

"Cornelia," said Kim, "you can't deny that in some places it's easier to be 'woman-identified,' as they so self-righteously put it."

"Stop it," said Mariette, "Stop bickering about who's more oppressed."

"They're the ones," said Barbara, filling everyone's wine glass, "who brand you with your personal life."

"But think of all the lesbians who are still in the closet," said Cornelia, feeling her body temperature rise ten degress, "who are afraid to lose their jobs."

"At our school?" laughed Rose. "At good old Progressive U?"

"The real stigma," said Barbara, "is the nepotism rule. Do you know how hard it is to be married to someone in the same field?"

"Yes," Kim began, "when I was at Hopkins. . . ."

Cornelia looked closely at the faces of her friends, her colleagues, her sisters and wondered how well she knew them, despite all the committee meetings and potlucks and commiserating drinks. Sometimes she felt like a hypocrite for not coming out to them. Other times she was sure they all knew. But for five years she had been silent. ("Self-protective," she called it. "Paranoid," charged Ruth. "Reserved," said Karen. "Sensible," said Mariette, who was now monitoring her every breath.)

"They just won't let you be a feminist," said Rose. "Heterophobia, I call it. Unless you wear a flannel shirt and . . ." she paused, not wanting to sound too bizarre, "handcuffs or something. . . ."

Cornelia cleared her throat.

Mariette watched fearfully.

"You just don't understand," Cornelia began.

"Yes," interrupted Mariette, desperate to swerve her friend from self-destruction. "That's like calling blacks 'racists.' "

Cornelia could hear her own fear in Mariette's voice. And this woke her to the absurdity of hiding political choice from her allies.

"You don't understand," she said. "*I* am a lesbian." Cornelia's eyes met Barbara's for a moment before her friend became absorbed by a speck in her wine glass. "I am one of those dyke feminists and I haven't kept you from anything." She saw Rose inch away toward the wall. "If I had so much power, I would have come out years ago." She noticed the quavering in her voice and the shaking of her glass, which she set on the table. Looking around, she found Mariette was the only one looking at her.

"I think what Cornelia's done is very brave," said Mariette.

"Oh, yes," said Rose. "I know how you feel. Remember when I lived with that heroin addict for a while? The stigma, I understand stigma."

"And discreet," said Barbara. "We've known you for four, five years! It's a real tribute to your social skills."

"How about a real indictment of social prejudice," said Mariette bitterly.

"Of course, in the larger academy," said Rose. "But among us, well, I'm sure we all would have, well, sympathized."

Cornelia's migraine had reached her right eyebrow.

The garden doors opened, admitting the hatted woman.

"I mean," said Kim, lowering her voice, "it's not like you're really one of them."

EXILE

Cheryl Ann Alexander

IMAGINE A GLOOMY March day in late-fifties New York. Up in Harlem, people hustle through the early afternoon cold to stand in line in supermarkets, as they do every Saturday, for the privilege of buying stale bread at a price one penny higher than what it sold for on East 85th Street when it was fresh. In one of the soot-ingrained tenements at the western end of 125th Street near Amsterdam Avenue, Laura Didier is preparing to do her weekly grocery shopping. A stocky woman in a gray wool skirt and black cardigan over a pink cotton blouse, she clumps around the combination kitchen-dining room in her rubbers, opening the doors of the cupboards over the sink and skirted washtub, making a mental grocery list. The eyes surveying the half-empty shelves are dark brown and set deep in the hollows between the strong forehead and high cheekbones. Those cheekbones, along with her copper complexion and proud nose, had caused one of the doctors at the arthritis clinic to ask if she was an American Indian. In fact, her features are quite characteristic of the ethnic blend of her native Trinidad, where Spanish adventurers and French planters had mingled blood with African slaves and their descendants for many generations. Her face, once arrestingly attractive, is now haggard. It sags under the full head of wavy gray hair parted on the left side and restrained by a fine net.

"Ma, Julia should be here any minute now. She said she'd come around two o'clock." The voice came from the living room and belonged to Laura's thirteen-year-old daughter, Anne.

"Yes, I know, Annie." Laura's voice had the God-grant-me-patience tone that mothers sometimes use, but she smiled briefly as she answered.

For weeks Anne had been living for this day when one of her classmates was to visit her and bring a record player and Elvis Presley records. Laura could not remember the last time she had seen Anne so excited; not for the visits of the two old nuns from her grade school who came dutifully twice a month, and certainly not for the daily visits of the teacher sent by the Board of Education to keep her abreast of her schoolwork.

Laura was ready. She stood in the doorway of the oversized closet which masqueraded as a living room. Anne lay on the couch reading a fan magazine. There were more fan magazines, Elvis Presley scrapbooks, and paperback books on the coffee table, which was pushed up against the couch. The pink quilted robe Anne's aunt Louise had given her for Christmas came down to her bobby-soxed ankles, but the bulkiness of her torso betrayed the presence of the plaster cast that hugged it from armpit to thigh.

How long she is, Laura thought. She will be tall like her father, tall and straight now that the curvature is corrected. Laura remembered the anguish she felt when, on a visit to Trinidad, a cousin had remarked that Anne seemed to be listing to one side. At first, she tried not to see it. But watching Anne running down the beach at Mazanilla or standing quietly looking out the window at Belmont, there was no denying it: her spine was curved. When did it happen? Why had she not noticed it herself—and sooner? Anne had been a perfect baby, a well child, completely healthy except for measles, chicken pox, and an occasional cold. Now this.

Laura had rushed Anne back to New York and into a frantic round of visits to orthopedists, physical therapists, chiropractors, and even faith healers. Finally, at Columbia Presbyterian Medical Center, Anne had undergone the spinal fusion from which she was now recovering.

"Do you want me to stay with you until she comes, Annie?"

"No, Ma, I can let her in myself. If you meet her on the way down, just tell her it'll take me a while to get to the door, so she should cool it after she rings the bell."

Laura suppressed a smile. The dear little ape. To hear her talk, you'd think she'd been born an American.

"All right, but be sure to ask 'Who is it' before you open the door. You can't be too careful in this place."

"Sure, Ma."

Laura went down the narrow entrance hall and pulled the string to turn on the bare light bulb in the ceiling. She rested her pocketbook on the clothes hamper under the oval mirror and took her black winter coat from its peg. As she put on her coat and hat, she examined her face in the mirror. So here I am at forty-eight, old— ancient, it seems, by American standards.

"You were thirty-five when Anne was born?" the social worker had asked incredulously.

"Yes."

"And she was your first child?"

"First and only."

Sighing softly, Laura pulled off the light and felt her way down the rest of the hall to the door. Unlocking the door, she called back to Anne, "I probably won't be back till around four o'clock. You know how crowded it is on Saturdays."

"O.K. Don't forget the ice cream."

"I won't, Anne. Strawberry. You've reminded me at least twelve times since you woke up this morning. Bye, bye."

"Bye, Ma."

Laura locked the door and, taking shallow breaths as protection against the smell of urine in the hallway, descended the three flights to street level.

In the vestibule stood three men. One of them, a mulatto with the florid discoloration of the alcoholic beneath his skin, greeted her, "How d'ye do, Miz Laura."

"Hello, Stanley," she said, recoiling from the stench of cheap wine on his breath.

The man standing next to him was a dark-skinned Negro with processed hair and expensive clothes. The faint freshness of his cologne mingled with Stanley's dank odor as he flashed Laura a brilliant smile and said, "Is a five, Miz Laura. Hope that's good news to you."

"I don't think so, Booker," she replied, determined to keep

distance between herself and the numbers runner.

The third man was a wizened octogenarian who lived on the second floor. He stood in a corner of the vestibule away from the other two. He tipped his hat to her, and Laura nodded.

"Mr. MacFarlane," she said as she opened the street door.

Hunching her shoulders, Laura went out into the freezing wind. She half-ran, half-walked the two blocks to A&P, but still her fingers were stiff and bloodless when she got there. She had to take off her gloves and rub her hands together for a few minutes before she could grasp the handle of a shopping cart. God, I hate winter, she cried out in her tropical soul. Why did I come to this cold country? But she knew why she had come.

She fled Trinidad when the man she had loved for thirteen years chose to ignore her and his child. The pain of existence on the same island with him was unbearable. It was a small island; everybody knew her. She would walk down the street under the blazing tropic sun and feel people pitying her, laughing at her. All the familiar foliage of her beloved homeland was rendered grotesque by her torment. Every flaming blossom on the immortelle tree seemed to be shouting, "Fool, he never loved you!" The thud of a ripe mango when it fell from the tree sounded like, "Fool!" She had to get away.

She had not known about the other women he'd been seeing all along until she found the letters. The words squirmed on the page like maggots on meat as she read through her tears.

"George, I would have expected a lover of mine to be far more shrewd in such matters, but I suppose if Laura is pregnant, you must marry her." This from Mary Roche in 1944 when she was four months pregnant with Anne and dismayed by his reluctance to set a wedding date. Not just Mary, but Doreen Laval, Annette Tobias, and Joan de Peza—they had all known about her and been jealous of her. She, on the other hand, had known that they existed, but had never dreamed that she shared her lover with them. She had been denied even the release of jealousy.

In New York, Laura lost all ambition. Shortly after her arrival, her sister Louise took her to work with her in the dress factory, and she stayed—she who had been one of the brightest young teachers in Trinidad. Nothing really interested her in this strange, cold city of pigeon-coop houses and gutteral diction, where everyone who wasn't white was black and condemned to Harlem. One feature of New York held a morbid fascination for her: the subway. On winter mornings as she stood on the platform of the Independent line, she marveled at the trains. What perfect suicide weapons they were! There was no chance of surviving being run over by one of these steel monsters which tore through the bowels of the city, screaming electric fury. She could end her misery with one short leap from the platform. But why give George the satisfaction? She would live on and never consent to a divorce. Besides, there was her child who was already fatherless; she could not make her motherless too.

Anne arrived in New York shortly after her sixth birthday. Laura had to blink when she saw the little girl who came shyly toward her along the ramp at La Guardia Airport. In three years she had changed from a baby to a female miniature of George: the same petulant mouth, the identical hazel eyes, the upturned nose, the high forehead, and the kinky hair, lots and lots of it.

Laura had had mixed feelings about bringing Anne to the United States. She knew that the child would probably be safer and happier growing up in Trinidad. Her grandparents had carved a secure niche for the family in the genteel society of Trinidad. They were considered a "good coloured family." And yet, Laura wanted Anne near to her. Why should her mother and sister get all her child's affection? She needed the child's warmth to keep her from turning into stone, a stone which could easily slip off the subway platform and be crushed. So she had sent for Anne, and not a day too soon; for although the child had obviously been well coached by her aunt and grandmother, Laura could tell that she really did not remember this mother who had flown away three years before.

Laura sent Anne to the Catholic grade school minutes away on 126th Street. She had been going to a small private school in Trinidad since age four, so the nuns placed her in the third grade with children at her level of scholastic achievement, but two years older. Anne was big for her age, and she met the challenge well. However, she was soon in trouble with both her teachers and her classmates.

"She's a little rascal," Sister Marie Regina told Laura during a conference called to discuss Anne's sticking her tongue out at the good Sister.

The few white students in the school didn't know what to make of her; the Negro kids figured it out immediately:

"You think you're better than everybody else, you ol' West Indian monkey!"

But Anne quickly acquired the passport to assimilation. Within two years of her arrival, she was fluent in the argot of her classmates — and very pleased with herself. She would grin delightedly as her mother strained to understand and correct.

"Dis lunch hour when we wuz all lined up to go in . . ."

"We *were* lined up, Anne."

"Go 'haid dere, Mama! Well, these public school cats bop by and start calling out to dis eighth grade cat, Albert Brisbane. Say 'Hey Pisspan! Hey Albert Pisspan!' We all got so tickled. I la-aughed myself."

"What did Sister Magdalena say?"

"Oh, she tried t' play it cool, 'tend she ain't heard nothin', see. But that chick's face wuz re-ed!"

Laura was disturbed by this development, but she need not have been. Anne graduated from eighth grade at the age of eleven. Her scores on the entrance examination were high enough to get her into the best Catholic girls' high school in New York. There her speech pattern changed again to match that of the middle-class white girls who constituted ninety-nine percent of the student body.

Anne was the only colored girl in her section of the freshman class. She often came home bubbling with stories about things that had happened at school; but Laura noticed that her friendship with these girls ended at three p.m. They never invited her to their homes or called her on the telephone; they never went places together. So this was the invisible color barrier. Laura had heard about it in Trinidad and had often wondered why any self-respecting colored person would want to live in such a country. When, in the throes of her grief, she fled to that very country, she had numbly accepted the *de facto* Jim Crow of New York. It seemed just one more drop in the ocean of her despair. She had kept to herself, shunning even the company of her compatriots.

There was a sizable population of West Indians in New York. They lived interspersed among the Negroes of Harlem, but socialized only among themselves. There were many people from Trinidad, even some from "good coloured families," but, except for her sister Louise, Laura's contacts with them were minimal. She avoided them for the same reason she'd left Trinidad: they all "knew."

Louise kept up with all the doings of the West Indian community. She attended all the gala "fetes" which the Trinidadians threw on even the most minor holidays. In her capacity as older sister, she often scolded Laura about her reclusive way of life.

"Why you don't go out and meet people? Why you only cooping up yourself in the house? What happen to you?"

Laura, cringing at the overdone American drawl with which Louise garnished her vehement Trinidadian dialect, would falter, "These people know my situation . . ."

"So what? They know too that you not the first woman to have a man leave her, and you won't be the last. They don't hold that against you."

"Lou, I can't. I just can't bring myself to . . ."

"What? You going to grieve for that no-good scamp for the rest of your life? You can't bring yourself to even dance with another man? Is the most ridiculous thing I ever hear! And you the one who got all the education!"

"Education has nothing to do with it."

"So I see."

At other times, Laura would hide behind Anne. "I can't leave the child by herself to go to parties."

"Leave her with Gladys," Louise would counter.

"I can't keep imposing on Gladys. She's good enough to keep her for me after school—"

"What you mean, 'She good enough'? You pay her."

"Yes but—"

"Yes, and she only too glad to make some extra money keeping her one or two Saturday nights every once in a while. Anyway, Anne not going to be a child forever. Three, four years from now, who will be her beaus? These numbers runners and dope pushers here in Harlem?"

"Don't be absurd, Louise."

"Well then, who?"

"When the time comes, I'm sure Anne will have lots of beaus."

These conversations always ended in an impasse. Louise would throw up her hands and flounce out. Laura would remain convinced that Louise could not possibly understand how she felt because she had never been married or even, Laura was certain, seriously in love.

Ignoring Louise's exhortations, Laura became settled in her monotonous existence. She spent her evenings helping Anne with her homework. They went to the library regularly, and sometimes mother and daughter would read aloud to each other. Occasionally, she would take Anne to a movie in the neighborhood or to Radio City Music Hall.

Anne had her first period a week before entering the hospital. After duly initiating her into the mysteries of the goddess Kotex, Laura had said, "Now you are a young lady."

"What's that supposed to mean?" Anne asked in her brash American manner.

"Well, if you were in Trinidad, it would mean that you would soon start going to the socials at George VI Hall."

"What's so great about that?"

"Oh, they're very nice dances for young ladies and gentlemen from good families."

"I can't dance."

"But you would learn. Most girls learn at your age."

"Well, there's no George VI Hall here," Anne had said wistfully. "But they have dances at school. The Halloween Hop is coming up. Joan was talking about it at lunch today."

"You'll be in the hospital," Laura said quickly, and steered the conversation to the coming operation, hoping that Anne had not noticed her uneasiness.

But the question of her daughter's social life had dogged her thoughts ever since that conversation. Now, as she headed for the checkout lanes, it sawed through her brain like a Calypso refrain. She nosed her cart into the space behind a Puerto Rican woman with a four-year-old hanging on to her coat and prepared for at least a twenty minute wait. She glanced at her watch—3:15. Then she remembered the strawberry ice cream. Her eyes ransacked the shopping cart, but it wasn't there. She realized that, lost in her thoughts, she had instinctively picked up only those items which she bought week after week. Strawberry ice cream was not one of them. It was a special occasion treat.

This really is a special occasion, she thought as she maneuvered her cart out of the line and aimed it at the dairy freezer along the back wall of the store. Anne had not seen girls from her high school since six of them visited her in the hospital. Julia Morgan had not been in that group, which had been a delegation from Anne's home-room. Julia, Laura gleaned, was in another of the three sophomore sections. But the nuns had urged all three sections to pray for Anne's recovery and send her cheering letters. Julia's first letter had been among the dozen or so waiting on the coffee table when Anne came home from the hospital. Anne had answered them all, but received only a trickle of replies, among them Julia's. The corres-pondence blossomed when the two girls discovered they were both Elvis Presley fans. Laura read some of the letters surreptitiously one day—pure adolescent drivel about his eyes, his hair, his voice and, of course, they were both going to marry him someday.

In keeping with the unwritten rule, there had been no phone calls between the two. So Laura was taken by surprise when Anne announced that Julia would be coming to visit with her entire col-lection of Elvis Presley records and the phonograph to play them on.

"Where does she live?" Laura had asked incredulously.

"Somewhere in Queens. Bay Ridge, I think."

"And she's going to bring records and a record player all the way over here on the subway?"

"No, Ma, her father's going to drive her over. They have a car."

"Does she know where you live?"

"She's got the address."

That sounded final to Laura. She had doused her skepticism and thrown herself into cleaning the apartment. It would have to be immaculate for the visit. She had also silently resolved not to tell Louise about the visit until after it had taken place. Louise had been wary of the whole Elvis Presley phenomenon from the beginning.

"Now tell me," she said to Laura one day, "why you let that child get carried away with this Elvis Presley nonsense?" It was more a challenge that a question. Laura was annoyed, but she affected nonchalance.

"I don't think she's any more carried away with it than any

other girl her age."

"Which other girls you know that have Elvis Presley scrapbook, and putting the radio up to their ear when his songs come on, and all that?"

"They show girls on television all the time, screaming at his concerts, kissing his pictures, dancing to his music. Haven't you seen it?"

"Yes, I see it. I also see that those are all white girls."

"Oh, Louise!" Laura was exasperated. "You're carrying this race business too far. You're becoming obsessed with it the way the American Negroes are. An adolescent girl is an adolescent girl whether she's black, white, brown, green, or blue."

"Not in *this* country they not," Louise said, wagging her head and glaring at Laura.

"I'm glad you're such an authority on this country," Laura said sarcastically.

"I been here longer than you. I go around, I see things, I talk to people," Louise said, nostrils flaring as she brought her fist down firmly on Laura's dining room table.

"Yes, your wonderful American friends."

"You can look down your nose at them if you want, but one thing I learn from them: In this country, it don't matter who you are or where you come from, if you black, you black."

To which Laura replied frostily, "Well you may do as you please, but I have no intention of forgetting who I am or where I come from. But we were talking about Anne."

"We still talking about her," said the unshakable Louise. "She must learn to adapt to the ways of this country. You not teaching her to adapt, and she won't learn it in that fancy white school you sending her to."

"Louise, I have no intention or reducing Anne's self-esteem or limiting her scope in any way. As far as I'm concerned, her only limits are her natural abilities."

"All right, have it your way; but if she was my child, I would make her wise up. Music and dancing is good, but with her own people."

"But she's not your child, Louise."

This exchange had had an insidious, unsettling effect on Laura.

Now, back in line, with the half gallon of Bryer's strawberry occu-pying a place of honor in the cart next to the stew beef, she looked around her. All the faces were Negro or Puerto Rican. Four of the six checkers were white; two were light-skinned Negroes. Laura remembered the stories she had heard in Trinidad about the Amer-ican South—bathrooms marked "White" and "Colored." Here nothing was marked; nothing need be said; everyone understood. Except my daughter. I really should have talked to her, explained to her long ago.

Laura was now up to the cash register. She was seized with a strange anxiety. Transferring her groceries from shopping cart to counter with nervous little jerks, she managed to force a joyless showing of the teeth which passed for a smile when the checker said, "How are you today?" She couldn't concentrate. Ordinarily, she would watch every price as it was rung up to be sure the checker didn't overcharge her. Today, she didn't care. She did remember, as she handed over the money, to ask him to divide the weight evenly between two bags.

In the vestibule between the store's inner and outer doors, she was met by a chorus of need-any-help-Ma'am's from the five or six boys huddled there. Hugging a bag in the crook of each arm, she ignored them and pushed open the outer door with her shoulder.

The wind had died down, and it was starting to snow—wet snow, the kind she hated most. Laura picked her way carefully, taking short running steps like a coolie carrying a heavy load on the wharf in Trinidad. It was impossible to see her watch, but she guessed that it was very close to four. I must have a long chat with Anne after dinner, after Julia leaves, she thought, and somehow the thought spread a formless panic through her being.

Stanley was alone in the vestibule. He opened the door for her. Laura's usual routine was to place her bags on the radiator, take off her gloves, warm her hands, and get out her keys. Now, she swept past the wino and up the stairs. At the third floor landing, breath-less, she put the bags down in front of the apartment door. Pulling off her gloves as if they were on fire, she rummaged frantically in her pocketbook for her keys. With one motion, she turned the key in the lock and pushed open the door.

"Annie! Annie!" she called as she dragged the bags inside and shut the door. For an infinite second she leaned against it. The apartment was still as an empty church. She swallowed. Resolutely, she turned the knob and heard the deadbolt fall to. She ran down the hall to the living room door.

Anne lay on the couch almost exactly as Laura had left her. Laura stood in the doorway.

"Has she gone already? Did you enjoy the visit?"

No answer.

Laura rushed into the living room and knelt beside the couch, knocking some magazines off the coffee table in her haste. Anne was crying. Her eyes were shut in an effort to keep in the tears which forced their way through the black lashes and rolled down her cheeks into her ears and hair and onto the green upholstery of the couch.

"Oh, darling, what's wrong? What happened?"

"She didn't come." Anne's face contorted as she wailed the words.

"Well, did she call up to say why?" Even as she uttered the question Laura saw how foolish it was.

The only possible answer came. "No."

Laura, crouching next to the couch, leaned over and pressed her cheek to Anne's saying, "Oh, honey, don't cry. Something must have happened. Maybe the car broke down or something."

"No," Anne said, "I think her father wouldn't bring her when he found out I'm colored and live in Harlem." Anne began to sob.

Laura, still pressing her cold cheek to her child's warm wet one, held Anne's head in both her hands. She thought of many things to say, but discarded them all before they passed her lips. She too began to cry. Old wounds opened. *I would have spared you this, my daughter. I wanted many brothers and sisters for you, and a warm home on the island where you were known and loved from the womb. But he would not.*

Anne was struggling to say something through her sobs. Laura listened.

"Ma, why are they like that?"

"I don't know, sweetheart. I don't think they do either."

"I'm not ever going to talk to Julia again when I go back to school."

"Darling, darling, I know how you feel. I know," Laura murmured,

"We were going to have so much fun."

"Wait, love, wait. You will have fun," Laura soothed. Comforting, crying, she willed love to soften anguish.

The doorbell rang, startling them. Sighing, Laura kissed Anne and rose stiffly. She strode down the dark hall to the door. No need to question the caller. Only one person rang the bell like that. She pushed the bags of groceries aside with her foot and opened the door. The shaft of fluorescent light from the hall fell on her swollen eyes and tear-stained face.

"Wh — what happen to you?"

"Hello, Louise. Come in, come in. You're letting in the cold."

CHUCK

Ruth Geller

BILL SAID HIS FRIEND Madeline knew everthing about dogs, and when we had trouble mating our Dalmatians, he phoned her for advice. Neither Bill nor I had ever handled mating and we hardly knew each other, having met one day at the vet's. We'd exchanged phone numbers, and when my Dalmatian went into heat I called him and we worked out the business part: I would pay him $150 for the use of his stud to impregnate my bitch. We'd both done some reading and knew that it wasn't the best idea to mate two inexperienced dogs, but he asserted that his male was always after females in the park. I told him that I was checking my female's fluids, and would call him when I thought she was ready. In the abstract, it was all quite simple.

When we actually got the dogs together in my back yard, however, they were more interested in playing than mating, and that's when we went into my kitchen and Bill phoned Madeline. After he spoke to her he relayed her opinion (that my female might not be ready) and her advice (that we bring the dogs to her house on Saturday). I shrugged and said it sounded good, but I would have to check a few things first; and while Bill stationed himself in the doorway and pretended that he was not inspecting the kitchen, I phoned Bernice at work. The number was busy.

"How long have you lived here?" Bill asked.

"Oh . . . 'bout five years," I said, and dialed again.

He nodded slowly, continuing his inspection. There is nothing so extraordinary about our kitchen or, for that matter, our house, except that from the outside, being a cottage without cellar or attic, it gives the feeling of impermanence, while the interior feels like a solid home.

"You married?" he asked.

"Uh . . . not exactly," I answered, and spoke into the phone: "Jo? It's Sue, will you try to drag Bernie away from that machine for a minute?" Bill was looking at me, but as soon as I met his eyes, he looked away. "You want a cup of coffee?"

He shook his head.

Bernice says I'm evasive, but I'll always answer a direct question; I merely can't abide the kind of gauging and measuring I felt from Bill, as though he could define me by my cannister set or the newspaper clippings on my refrigerator. Since I work first shift and Bernice works second, the way we communicate during the week is to leave little clippings, things we think the other person will enjoy. There is nothing terribly personal about them; they are, after all, in the kitchen, and I never mind when people read them since it gives me a chance to talk about Bernice. Most of the time people walk right up to the refrigerator, but Bill was straining his eyes from across the room, glancing at me to see if I noticed. Nonchalantly I moved in front of the refrigerator, blocking his view.

Finally Bernice came to the phone. "Bernie, is the Center cookout this Saturday or next, I forgot to write it down . . ."

Bill was looking at his fingernails.

"Okay, I've got something to do, I'll explain later, so will you make the potato salad? Fine, then I'll take the car, and soon as I get back, we can go . . . Mm-hmm . . . Okay, sweetie, see you tonight . . . No, I'll probably be up . . . See you later." I hung up. "Okey doke, it's all set."

We returned to the yard. I made a joke to the effect that if we found the dogs lying in the shade smoking cigarettes, we'd know everything was all right. Bill didn't crack a smile. He said that we'd have to mate the dogs twice in any case, and getting them together now would save time. I agreed it would be nice if the dogs mated today, but balked at the suggestion that we position them. His jaws clenching with impatience, he looked at his watch and began to cite the various books he'd read that recommended . . . blah blah blah . . .

and I agreed, unable to withstand the onslaught of his logic, but thinking to myself: 'You uptight bastard, she's *not ready*.'

The expression on my face indicated that I knew positioning the dogs was not going to work, and I would do as he'd argued merely to prove him wrong. "Okay, pooch," I explained to my dog as I anchored her body between my knees, "this is just a little experiment." I petted her head gently while Bill, looking determined but harassed, grasped his male's front legs from behind and tried to mount the one dog on top of the other. I hoped to God that none of my neighbors were watching. The dogs didn't seem too happy about the situation either, and in fact, looked distinctly embarrassed. It was finally clear even to Bill that they were not going to, as he'd urged, "get down to business," and we released them, agreeing to meet at Madeline's on Saturday.

Saturday morning I lured Sophie Tucker, my fertile Dalmatian, into the car with a scrap of bologna, wrapped the rest in a piece of newspaper, stuck it in my pocket, and drove to Madeline's.

She lived in a suburban tract house, and when I reached the block of lookalike square structures, I had a vivid mental picture of her; but when I saw her house I decided I might have been wrong. In a neighborhood where people had planted polite back yard barriers of forsythia and privet hedge, Madeline's yard was defined by a no-nonsense five foot chain link fence. The lawn in front needed mowing, especially in comparison to its crewcut neighbors. From among the ragged blades of grass, long yellow dandelions blared out rebelliously.

I pulled into the driveway and got out of the car, leaving Sophie inside. Four poodles in the back yard were yapping at me from behind the fence. I disliked their clipped unnatural appearance, and thought them neurotic-looking with their mean, narrow faces and weepy eyes, but feeling guilty about this irrational prejudice, I knelt down and let them sniff my hand.

From inside the house a voice yelled: "Come on in!" and I walked up the steps. Bill and Madeline were sitting at the kitchen table. Madeline, calling me by name, pulled out a chair and offered me a cup of coffee, and Bill, looking abashed, introduced us belatedly. Madeline poured the coffee and said we didn't need any introduction, we'd do fine on our own. She slid a carton of milk toward me and they continued their conversation about a mutual friend who bred Rottweilers, I waited for my coffee to cool, and observed Madeline.

She was a stout woman in her late forties, dressed in a loose-fitting cotton housedress with large square pockets. She was sitting back, legs slightly spread, hands resting on her thighs. Her stubby fingernails were painted a frosty white which had chipped in several places. On her legs grew a faint stubble of hair, and she wore an old pair of shoes that were cut at the little toe to accommodate her corns.

She looked at me. "Do you know Rottweilers?"

"No."

"They're the dogs they used in that movie *The Omen*," Bill said.

"Oh. I didn't see it."

"I only went to see it for the Rottweilers," Madeline said, laughing, and began to describe the breed. I pretended to listen, and looked at her face. In contrast to her body, her features were delicate. She'd painted a strip of frosty green eye shadow on the lids of her small blue eyes. Many people have dead eyes, shiny plastic orbs that are just another part of their machinery, but as Madeline spoke to me I sensed that I would learn more from her eyes than from her words. I sensed that the body and life in which she was contained defined little of who she really was. We smiled and turned away, she to Bill, and I to the kitchen in general.

It was decorated in an uncertain early American style. A ceramic plaque hung somewhat askew on the wall; within a Pennsylvania Dutch design were the words: "Too Soon Oldt und Too Late Schmart."

Madeline slapped both hands on the table, pushed back her chair and said: "Well, let's get on with it."

I brought Sophie down to a room in the basement where Madeline groomed poodles. Bill's dog Solomon was waiting. We watched from our various corners while the dogs sniffed each other, tails wagging. They were excited, but didn't know quite what to do.

"I wouldn't exactly call it passion in the basement," I said dryly, and Madeline burst out laughing. Bill was watching Solomon anxiously.

"*She's* ready," Madeline said, indicating Sophie's firm stance and her tail, held to one side to accommodate the male.

"He'll get the hang of it," Bill defended.

After awhile Madeline leaned against the counter near a copy of *Dog World*. "I think we all better settle down for a long wait."

"Come on, Solomon," Bill urged. "I don't understand it, in the park he's *always* after females."

"Oh relax, Bill, for goodness' sake, you'd think, it was *your* performance we're all waiting for." She looked at me, shaking her head, and I turned away smiling, not wanting to laugh outright. I wondered where her husband was, but realized that with a woman like her, the husband didn't matter. He might be working or fishing or dead. His occasional presence or past existence was merely decoration to appease society's critical eye.

Sophie stood immobile, back end toward Solomon, every so often looking over her shoulder at him. He sniffed here and there, tail wagging. Bill said, "He likes her, that's for sure."

"Of course," Madeline agreed, "it's natural. They just have to be taught how, that's all."

"Maybe they don't like to have an audience," I suggested.

"We'll see. If they don't get the hang of it, we'll give 'em a little boost." After a moment, Madeline picked up the Rottweiler conversation where they'd left off: "So then Polly came to see me and said, 'Madeline,' she said, 'who do you think I ought to get to stud for Cerise?'" Here Madeline looked meaningfully at Bill. He raised his eyebrows and smiled. "Well," she said, relishing his anticipation, "I would have told her to call Chuck, because his Phantom is *such* a beautiful animal. *But . . .*"

Bill nodded his agreement that she could not tell Polly to call Chuck, shook his head and tsk-tsked the entire situation. I wondered if perhaps Chuck's dog was a fraud, or Chuck an unscrupulous breeder.

Solomon was trying to mount Sophie's head. I turned away, laughing, "Oh my God . . ."

"Well, he's got the right idea," Madeline said.

"Yeah, just the wrong end."

Bill was rigid. "Come on, Solomon, come on . . ."

"Maybe we inhibit them," I said.

"Maybe," Madeline answered. She was looking at Sophie, and

soon began praising her. She found excellence in everything: the uniformity in size and color of her spots, their even distribution over her body, her dense glossy coat, the closeness of her elbows to her frame . . . Bill maintained a sceptical silence. I knew he didn't understand Madeline's enthusiasm, but I understood it quite well.

Women like her often strike up conversations with me in supermarkets and bowling alleys, talking about the price of lettuce or how they admire my followthrough, all the while looking into my eyes, not understanding and so not bothering to conceal their attraction. They are women of her generation, women who might have foregone the convention of a husband had not the convention been so strong. I stand and commiserate about the price of lettuce or find common ground in our bowling experience, all the while feeling a bond across the years.

After awhile Madeline's praise of Sophie embarrassed me, for I knew my dog to be a sweet but average Dalmatian. Apparently Solomon was also unimpressed with Sophie's spots and elbows, or else he'd given up, for he had gone over to the corner and lain down.

Upstairs, the back door slammed and we heard: "Ma! I'm home!"

"That'll be Audrey," Madeline said. "We might as well go upstairs and have some more coffee. Maybe you're right," she said to me, smiling, "maybe they're just shy."

As we left the dogs to themselves, Bill murmured: "It *is* too bad about Chuck . . ."

"I know. I liked him so much," she said sadly, latching the gate so that the dogs could not escape. "His poor family. That's what I keep thinking: his poor family."

"And he was so good with animals!" Bill said, and I half expected him to raise his fist to heaven and demand: Why did you cut him down in the prime of life!

I was convinced that Chuck had met with some tragic fate. A car crash, perhaps. Yes, that seemed the most likely thing. Maybe he was paralyzed. I walked up the stairs trying to imagine the trapped feeling of being able to move nothing but my eyes. One blink for yes, two for no. As I reached the top of the stairs I held my body stiffly, squeezing my eyes shut, popping them open in exaggerated blinks.

Opening my eyes on the last blink, I saw Madeline on the landing watching me. She smiled in toleration of whatever fantasy I had chosen to act out, and said: "Come and meet Audrey."

Audrey, a girl of about fourteen, was reaching into a ceramic cookie jar shaped like a rooster, and when Madeline entered the kitchen Audrey glanced immediately at her feet. Seeing those old shoes, a succession of expressions came over her face that seemed lifted straight out of a silent move: dismay, accusation, and (after Madeline said warningly, "Hello, Audrey") frustration, which she vented by devouring a cookie. Bill and I resumed our places at the kitchen table, and Madeline turned on the fire underneath the coffee pot.

Ignoring her mother, Audrey spoke to Bill. "Is Solomon downstairs?" she asked by way of greeting, and without waiting for his answer or her mother's introduction, turned to me. "You're the one with the other Dalmatian, right?"

"Right."

"How they doing?" she asked, long familiar with the facts of dog breeding.

"Well, they've vowed eternal friendship, but I'm afraid that's about all."

"Now don't you worry," Madeline said, "all in good time."

"Ma . . ." Audrey said with a childish whine that sounded like it was a ritual aspect of her conversation with her mother, "what time are we going to eat supper . . ."

"What time do we *always* eat supper," Madeline answered with a patience just as ritual.

"Well, I'm going over to Betsy's then," she said, and left abruptly with another slam of the door.

"That girl," Madeline said to me, "is either slamming doors or leaving them wide open. I can't wait until she meets a happy medium. How 'bout that coffee . . ."

"Sounds good to me," I said. It was nearing two o'clock and I was getting hungry. I'd left home having eaten neither breakfast nor lunch, assuming with my customary lack of foresight that if I was not hungry at noon, I would not be hungry at two. Sophie Tucker's return trip bologna was beginning to look appetizing.

Madeline poured the coffee and began speaking about a dog

show she'd attended last week. I paid no attention until I happened to glance at Bill. He was leaning forward expectantly, listening to Madeline who was saying: "And sure enough, at twelve fifteen, right before it begins, in walks Chuck with his 'friend' . . ."

"You're kidding," he pronounced.

She shook her head, delighted with the scandal. She saw that I was listening, and wanting to include me, said, "I don't know if you'd call it his 'boyfriend' or his 'girlfriend.' " Bill snickered, and Madeline asked me, "What would *you* call it . . ."

I remembered an incident I hadn't thought of in years. I'd gone to the hospital to visit a friend who was dying of cancer. The doctor came in to examine her, and I had to wait in the lounge, where another patient tried to make conversation with me, telling me about his operation. My thoughts were with my friend, and I responded to him indifferently. He tried one approach after another, and as I sat there, he began complaining about his hospital room-mate who had late night habits and early afternoon visitors. "I don't see where they get off coming in the middle of the day," he muttered, "don't those people work for a living? Probably half of 'em are on welfare . . ." Then, in a final effort to enlist my sympathy, he offered: "Goddamned niggers think the world owes 'em a living . . ."

Later I wondered how I would have responded to him had I not been so preoccupied with my friend's condition. But at that point my attention didn't focus on him until I became aware that he was staring at me. His eyes were crafty with sudden comprehension. Oh, so that was it, I was one of *those* . . . He stood up, directing, before he left, a long accusing glare at my traitorous white face.

Madeline was speaking again, and now she sounded betrayed: "I never would have figured Chuck for one. Of all people . . . Chuck!"

"He certainly didn't *look* like one," Bill observed.

"No, he didn't. And I always said I could spot them a mile off. He used to sit right here in this kitchen and drink coffee . . . Sometimes we'd talk for hours." She paused, and blurted: "I thought he was my friend, and all that time —"

Madeline stopped in mid-sentence; from behind the partially glassed door she'd seen Audrey eavesdropping greedily, a cunning expression on her face. Madeline looked urgently from the door to Bill and back again, but he was gazing down. "I know," he said thoughtfully. "Nobody could tell a joke like Chuck, and nobody could—"

"Why aren't you at Betsy's!" Madeine broke in.

Discovered, Audrey opened the door, trying to appear bored. "She had to do homework."

"Well then maybe you'd better go do yours."

"I will," the girl said, but wandered in our direction, trailing her finger across the counter top, adjusting the toaster a fraction of an inch to the side . . .

"Well!?" Madeline demanded.

Audrey whirled around and faced her mother with a pout calculated to wrench pity from the most hardened of hearts. "Can't I even get something to eat?"

Madeline folded her arms slowly across her chest. "Get something to eat. But don't dawdle."

Audrey floated around the kitchen, seemingly absorbed in the process of toasting an English muffin, a process so lengthy—she had to split the muffin just so, and choose a jam—that Madeline said, "Well, I'm going to see what I can do downstairs."

"Can I come?" the girl pleaded, suffering in advance because she knew the answer.

"No!"

"Aw, gee . . ."

I gestured to my coffee. "I'll be down in a minute."

Madeline disappeared downstairs with Bill, and as soon as she was gone, so was Audrey's pout. She set her muffin on the table and sat down across from me all businesslike: "Did you know Chuck?"

I shook my head and eyed her English muffin. She had separated it with a fork so that the tiny peaks were toasty crisp, the tiny valleys flooded with melted butter. I wondered if Bernice was making the potato salad. I thought again of that newspaper-wrapped bologna in my pocket, and wondered if I would learn something about the world if I ate cold-cuts imprinted with the news of the day.

"I met him," she bragged. "He used to come over *all* the time."

I nodded and watched her dip a teaspoon into a jar of strawberry preserves and spread the lovely red goo onto the muffin.

"He's a homo," she said, looking at me to see how I would react.

My first reaction was to laugh, for I remembered myself at about her age snickering at "homo" milk. I kept silent, not wanting her to think I was laughing at Chuck.

She observed my lack of reaction to the word, opened her mouth to redefine it, and changed her mind. Since I was too dense to impress, she was no longer interested in my company. She gobbled down the rest of the jam-topped muffin with a speed that should have been criminal. "Oh well," she said and licked her fingers, "I'm off." She gathered her books and went upstairs. Soon I heard rock music and her accompanying "oh yeah"'s.

I was alone with an educated slice of bologna and a kitchen chock full of food. I was sorely tempted to sneak a peek in the cookie jar, and was considering the quietest way to open the crockery rooster's head when I heard a commotion in the cellar. I walked to the landing and saw Bill's stud on my bitch. I held my breath and started slowly downstairs. They were tied. Madeline gently turned the stud, and the three of us soothed and petted the dogs, waiting for them to come apart.

Bill left soon after, but Madeline kept me there for over an hour. She clipped Sophie's nails, complimenting me on her compact feet and well-arched toes. She insisted that I have more coffee, persuading me by the mention of her home-made coffee cake. As I ate she explained about vitamins, whelping boxes, false pregnancies, after-birth and breech births, all the while making excuses to touch me: taking a sweater off the back of my chair, handing me a registration brochure from the American Kennel Club, and as a general emphasis to her statements. She did not want me leave. Each time I mentioned the hour, she renewed her efforts, found something to interest me and engage me.

She kept trying to define me through vague searching questions; but I, warned by Chuck's experience, refused to focus her search, pleasantly answering each inquiry as I would the police if I were harboring an outlaw.

As I finally made my way out the door, she repeated that I should call if we had any trouble with the second mating, call and let her know if the matings took, if my dog had any problems with the pregnancy, and certainly call her for the whelping itself. I was polite but more concerned that I didn't fall over Sophie, who was leashed and kept stepping in my path. The four poodles were yapping excitedly behind the fence. Madeline followed me out to the driveway, insisting on lending some puppy bottles in case my dog had problems nursing.

I protested, "But Madeline, shouldn't I wait to see . . . I mean there's no sense in . . ."

She cut me off with a wave of her hand. "You have to be prepared for every emergency," she said with a finality against which it was foolish to argue. While she went into the house, I lured Sophie into the car with the bologna, and got behind the wheel. Madeline came out carrying an armload of small plastic bottles, nipples attached. She had to see me again: whether or not I used the bottles, I would have to return them.

I appreciated her help with the mating and didn't want her to think me ungrateful, but I was wary; though she persisted in reaching out to me, I was unwilling to offer my own hand. I liked her, but I did not want my fingers crushed when her mind slammed against me as it had against her friend Chuck.

She was still watching as I drove away. In the rear view mirror I saw her standing in the driveway. Her hand was positioned midway between a beckoning and a farewell. Her mouth was half open as though her heart wanted to call me back but her mind did not know the words.

THE SURVIVOR

Janice Mirikitani

FUMI SAID IT WASN'T worth it.

If she had to give up smoking, it simply wasn't worth it. The doctor had told her it would certainly cut down the odds against her if she would give them up. She wouldn't. If she was in control of nothing else, it would be her own slow death. She couldn't give them up . . . especially now with a new position opening. She wanted it, and she waited so long for it. Eight years of seniority, impeccable work record. No absences. In eight years Fumi didn't miss a day except to go to her mother's funeral. Frail mama, who managed to live to be eighty-two.

> *You gotta be a Survivor,*
> *Fumiko. They'll try to whip*
> *you down, but don't you flinch.*
> *Never let them see*
> *you're hurt*
> *or afraid.*
> *Just keep standing straight*
> *turn your back,*
> *let the lash fall*
> *without twitching.*

> I gotta tell you, Mama.
> You're pretty hard on me . . .

driving, whining,
whipping me with guilt.
I'm not taking away
what you gave me
but you really
were a pain in the ass.
I'm burying you,
but your ghost, thin
as bamboo
still hangs over
the furo,
elbow crooked
for me to hold you up.

Fumi lit a cigarette. All she had to do was wait . . . the new job
shone in her mind like a tunnel's end. She worked hard . . . self-
imposed discipline, to soothe her feeling of invisibleness. She was a
taut wire of work to defend against cobalt eyes and ice-white walls
of flesh.

Mama, I gotta give it
to you. You were a
Survivor.
You turned that rock farm
into strawberries.
And when they took us
to the camps,
you didn't look back once.
Eyes dead ahead,
dripping big like berries.
The sun
that day
was like no other
rotting in an orange sky.
It dried up the world
like an apricot pit
hard . . . bitter . . .
The world they sent us to

Amache Gate*
A gate slammed shut
one way.
The ground there was ungiving.
No dirt, no sand
just dust that blew
into our pores.
I can't forget, Mama.
The guards were making bad jokes
at our backs
about low built barracks
for low built japs.
Those barracks —
mocking us, row after row,
in the dust.

Fumi lit another cigarette. Mr. Dogett should be calling any day now.

Erma sat at a desk across the office, giggling into the phone. Erma with the dyed strawberry-blond hair which she had set and styled every Friday morning, so she always came in late on Fridays. What'd the doctor say, Fumi? Did he tell you how smoking causes wrinkles, especially those around your mouth and eyes, huh? Did he tell you how every time you take a puff one cell dies from suffocation, huh? Fumi? And how your skin turns yellow, huh? Oh . . . ya know . . .

Erma was looking into her compact mirror, pushing up her eyebrows with her spit-wet pinky. Erma reeking of La Interdet perfume.

Fumi lit another cigarette.

You know I want to
throw up, don't you, Mama.
How you would nag me

---

* Amache Gate: One of the ten concentration camps in which over 110,000 Americans of Japanese ancestry were incarcerated during World War II.

about smoking.
about my hairstyles, my weight,
my clothes, my smelling
like lifebuoy soap and cigarettes.
It's not their imitation French
perfume, the spun sugar hair,
corsets and deodorants
that make this vomit curl
in my throat,
it's the way they walk
around me . . . clear around me,
like I am the clock or the desk.
I can't forget, Mama.
You had already peed once
on yourself because the bus refused
to stop for anything but gas.
And then they wouldn't let us out.
You made me cover you with my coat,
hot as it was, so the smell
wouldn't offend anyone else.
I couldn't wash the ghost
of your smell from my coat.
I was worried about you, Mama
not being so young, and after
that long train ride, too.
When we finally got there
we rushed to the toilets
naked, wall-less, stall-less.
Holding you up by the elbow
you peed
right next to Mrs. Fujihara
and turned to each other
and apologized.

Fumi lit another cigarette. Erma pulled out a lace-bordered handkerchief and held it delicately to her nose. I saw a documentary once about customs around the world, ya know? Gee Fumi, I didn't know they send Japanese girls into the ocean to gather up

oysters, huh? While the men sit on the beaches under big umbrellas
and fan themselves, huh, Fumi, huh? They just sit there, all day,
watching their women like fish diving again and again for pearls,
huh? What do those men do to you if you come up oysterless? Huh?
Fumi? huh?

Fumi lit another cigarette.

> I want to throw up.
> I know you told me never
> to lose my temper, Mama.
> It's undignified. Don't show
> them what we feel. Don't give
> them the edge.
> But Mama, they don't even care.
> If they would give me the coarse
> texture of hate
> the taut fibre of their fear
> the solid stuff of anger —
> that would be human.
> It's the indifference
> I can't fight.
> Maybe your fight was too real, Mama.
> Papa was so mad.
> There was no more sugar —
> they would take even his
> last grain of pleasure.
> He stood at the space
> between the barrack
> and the fence that yawned his impotence.
> That tortuous space that dangled
> freedom like a dead fish.
> His legs twitching
> to take the stride to the edge.
> We could hear the guard's
> rifle cock click.
> OTOSAN!!
> Kicking the dust through space
> hurling it like a fist

veins popping
from his neck as he raged.
Raged.
Raged against the cold
steel, silent wire.

Fumi lit another cigarette. Erma applied fresh lipstick, called
"pouting pink." Get the phone, huh, Fumi. I just smeared my lips.
Harold wouldn't ever let me lift a finger, ya know? I'm only working cause I got bored, right? American men are so good to their
women, huh, Fumi? You should find you a man, now that your
mother's gone, ya know, huh, Fumi? Not getting any younger, huh?
That nice Japanese pharmacist down on 2-East, Mr. Ching, uh
Chong, er Chow, huh Fumi?
Fumi lit another cigarette.

I think I'm really
going to throw up.
Mama, you tried so hard
picking all the right men for me.
A man with a profession is
good insurance, you said.
Well, Mama, there was a time
when I thought I would escape
you.
My loins afire with love;
a longing for him deeper than
the need for freedom.
He made me feel almost beautiful.
He was strong
didn't say much
but it was pleasure in those
silences and the laughter
in between.
You didn't like his family.
When he left to fight their war,
I really wanted to die,
there at Amache Gate, dust

picking at my nostrils
in the rotting afternoon.
Nothing but the sound of flies
on the dead ground.
He never came back to anywhere.
When his family heard the news
that came through the cruel,
late mail, his younger brother
ran from the barrack,
screaming, tearing at his face
right up to the fence, tearing
at the barbed wire.
Even the guards
turned their heads.

Fumi lit another cigarette. Erma was backcombing her hair. Guess what, Fumi? Mr. Dogett called me to interview for that new position, ya know? I think I'll get a new dress that really fits, huh? That'll impress him, huh, Fumi, huh? You really should stop smoking, Fumi, it'll turn your fingers yellow, ya know?

Fumi lit another cigarette.

God, Mama, I really miss you.

A HARDENED CASE

Evelyn Shefner

THE HOUR WE ARRIVED, only the big armored trucks were on the streets. Everyone in town was still asleep, or yawning and turning over for five luxurious minutes. The metal clapper on top of Ingersoll's Big Ben was puncturing dreams in bungalows and three-story brick apartment houses the width and breadth of Chicago. Lights were going on in bathrooms and kitchens; fingers were scratching or sullenly poking; patched bathrobes and stained kimonos were sitting down to breakfast.

The flat city stirred to life. Winds of necessity blew through courtyards, down alleys and boulevards. They carried me straight into the financial district, where the large armored trucks cruised, dropping off, picking up cloth bags handled by gun-toting guards. Past the Bank of the Midwest; past the Federal Savings and Loan; up La Salle Street—where I saluted gilded Ceres, on top the Board of Trade—they deposited me in a stuffy room inside Consolidated Utilities, where I spent the next eight hours figuring out the odds on escaping family disgrace.

We worked four to a table, four tables to a row. There must have been three hundred of us girls in all—it was a large, miscellaneous crew. When a girl read out loud from a particularly damning example she held up for the crowd to see, her voice might be heard by forty or fifty others, depending on where she was sitting and who was doing the shouting. Some of those who got singled out for attention were pretty scandalous cases: you'd think some people had nothing better to do than spend a lifetime deliberately baiting the Utilities Company by holding back payment.

Though the supervisors said we were lucky to be there, to tell the truth it was a job fit only for machines. Every customer-history-record card in the files for the Greater Chicago Area was in the process of being hand-copied and recoded—the job to be completed within twelve weeks, chop-chop. Where on the old cards a cut-off for nonpayment might be marked "XX," on the new ones it was shown for instance by "OO." As I remember, there were codes for monthly arrears, a code for a First, a Second, a Final Notice Before Shut-off. A code for Reinstatement of Services. For chronic, repeated offenders, a secret code marked in red at the top of the card.... A lifetime of poor management could be compressed on one of these dog-eared, fading records.

"Listen to this one, girls! Goldberg, Aaron, Douglas Boulevard. Twenty electric cut-offs, sixteen gas cut-offs *in the past three years.* A total, let's see, thirty-six. I think that hits the record so far."

"Here, wait, I've got a better. Goldman, Isidore"—already we were well into the G's. "There's a store with this one too, so the total comes to forty-three."

Could it be only Jews who got in trouble and couldn't pay their bills? Scratch a Chicagoan, I believed at the time, and you'd rub skin off an anti-Semite: the little Polish boys on their way home from parochial school had packed murderously efficient lumps of coal inside their snowballs. "Yid! Chickenfat! Go home and eat matzos."

"*Blood sausage!*"—to say it I never dared, but I developed an early proficiency at the zig and the zag, the feint and the dodge.

"Gold-stein, Ben . . ." This one was sitting too far away, but her voice-tone sank into the discouragement I felt when I came back to the dusty house in the late afternoons, and saw the hunk of koshering meat draining into the sink, waited for my sister's complaints, the baby's abandoned crying.

"How come you're home so early, Golda?"

"It's four-thirty. I only work till four—remember?"

"I've had so much to do all day, and the baby's throwing up his lunch—here, you hold him—I haven't been able to tell the time. . . . Sitting all day like a lady: you don't call that a job, do you?"

When my parents came back late from the store, somber and ravenous, we set grimly to work on the floury flanken, the burned tsimmes, the potatoes that rattled on the plate like marbles. We spooned up compote like people on the stage, pretending to enjoy; always either too sweet or too sour. — A cook like that, no wonder Marvin had walked out on her.

At the time, we were all in a state of semimourning, because it was the First Divorce in the Family. Even Bernice got the point, and for days didn't comb out the tight whorl of pincurls that hugged her scalp like a flattened wig. The baby got its little fingers scratched, trying to pull them out.

"How much longer is the job lasting you, Goldie?"

"I told you, Ma — it's supposed to go on until March 15."

My mother sighed and slumped lower over the ironing board, while Bernice sat by, applying nail polish with clumsy fingers. My father, unshaved and shoeless as usual, also slumped, in a chipped kitchen chair, but I felt his wilted encouragement reaching out to bolster my decision. He knew and I knew I was the youngest, and the all-time favorite.

"And after that, you'll be left without anything to do, like all summer and fall —. Remember what I told you, about Mrs. Bernstein's daughter? She got out of college, and still she took a course in bookkeeping."

"I admit," I said, "that the world isn't exactly turning itself over for English majors, but it's possible my day will come —"

"And what you're doing now, it's so much more interesting than being a bookkeeper?" Bernice asked, sardonically.

"It isn't. No, it's not, but the advantage, you see, is that it's temporary —"

"She calls that an advantage!" Bernice shrugged, and looked up at the ceiling. "Five years I worked, steady, without one day off, Depression or no Depression, before Marvin and I got married," she announced to no one who was interested in hearing. "And if I wasn't tied down right now, you'd see how I'd make waves — *if* I had someone to take care of the baby," she said, bending over to examine the rompers my mother was — at that hour of the night —

ironing.

"I can't leave the store." *She* slammed down the iron, and *he* grunted.

It was the first store they'd ever had where I wasn't expected to help out during my free time. A narrow oblong, a counter, a few shelves—it was so small there was hardly room for my father, my mother, and the occasional customer. Notions, dressmaking supplies: patterns, braid, snaps, ribbons, a few well-aged bolts of cloth. Every time I dropped by I shuddered, because it was exactly like the places widows set themselves up in, to give themselves something to do. The stock was so small he could easily have packed it up in a suitcase, and rung doorbells. I don't know why he went on paying rent. My mother went there every day chiefly to cheer the man up, and because seeing for herself how bad things were, she said, helped to cheer her up.

"Well, if you've got nothing to do after March," Bernice said hopefully, "maybe while you're home I could go out and find myself some—"

"I wouldn't count on it," I told her. "I might just skip town before that time," I said, thinking about the job. By then we'd mopped up the G's and were heading into the H's.

For a first job after college, I'd expected better: having to arrive at that hour on brisk Chicago mornings was no paid vacation. Pale-eyed Sue-Ellen, leader and inspector general of our little squadron of four, who might have expected better still, took the situation a lot calmer and more cheerfully than I. "It's a job that's got to get finished," she'd say, "so we might as well do the best we can. Fern, you're fine: but you, Golda, and Corrine"—she handed us back the work we'd bungled—"you've been letting a few errors slip by. The important thing is not to lie down on the job," she'd say, as my eyelids dropped, and I pinched myself under the table, leaving discernible bruises.

I was a graduate of a University said to have the best library West of Harvard—from my use of it, you'd never know—but Sue-Ellen had driven around her family's estate in childhood in a little goat cart. It seemed to me improbable anyone could have invented this baroque story. She'd had advantages, including boarding schools and trips to Europe and the Far East; following her father, a Daddy Warbucks sort of figure, who'd been active in minerals, or oil. Crossing first class, for pleasure, while the parents and grandparents of the people I knew had sweated it out in steerage, for grim necessity. Whatever the family enterprise, it must have collapsed, otherwise why should she be joining us those winter mornings, and glad to do it too?

"I'm perfectly satisfied to be here," Sue-Ellen would say, squinting at the cards in front of her, her whitish gray eyes practically invisible behind the thickness of her lenses. She was the first Gentile I'd ever met whose eyes were worse than mine. "It's the attitude you bring to anything that counts. I'd go out and scrub floors before I'd take money from the Government, like some of those idlers and New Deal shirkers."

You'd think That Man had just been elected to his first term in office: some people just couldn't lean back and accept the flow of events.

Conspiracies, Sue-Ellen would hint, were robbing The People of their birthright of initiative, by coddling and excessive spending: all in the interests of sinister overseas dogmas. Mistaken Government philanthropy was eroding the home-grown character, and ought to be abolished—

"You mean, you'd wipe out *social security*?" I lowered my voice, seeing heads turn.

"Last year," Sue-Ellen said primly, "they told me I was eligible for Unemployment, but I wouldn't touch it. Let the Reliefers and people who never pay their bills"—she rested her fingers on the card she was scanning—"stand in line to collect money they aren't entitled to."

"Well, they're entitled by law!"

"No one's entitled to a cent he hasn't worked for." She buried her face in a stack of cards, as the toilet bell rang.

Bells rang halfway through the morning, halfway through the afternoon, freeing us for a fifteen-minute pee-and-smoke break. The scheduled performances, gushing into the ladies' room like the the Buckingham Fountain show in Grant Park, were torrential. The half-hour lunch break was ushered in and broken off by bells. Prison guards—monitors—efficiency experts patrolled the aisles as we worked, glancing at their watches and keeping an ear out for gossips and habitual babblers. The only sounds they positively tolerated were those occasional outraged shrieks—"Mitchell, William!" "Nolan, Patrick!" (we were getting up in the alphabet), followed by the usual resumé of some poor householder's lifelong incapability or larcenous intent. The monitor would stop, look at her watch, smile, and wait for the tirade to be over before putting a finger to her lips. . . .

To me, they were all perfect little sadists, the sort who spend Sunday afternoons gaping through the bars at inmates on the grounds of mental institutions, and at the time I could not envisage one other person in the room waiting in sickness or resignation for her moment of truth to arrive. But given what the country had gone through in the recent past, was going through still, surely there must have been others: asking if the shrill heartless voice would ring out in her ears from just across the aisle, or worse, if her family's record would turn up—against the odds—at her own table. Considering the odds (unless some hidden form of selection had been at work), for instance was it likely that Fern Kahn, the only other Jewish girl I'd been able to recognize up there, should be placed shoulder-to-shoulder, next to me? Or given the even greater coincidence of our sharing the same last name, that Sue-Ellen and I should be exchanging views of life every day across a metal worktable?

Speaking of names: Golda simply got my goat. It was its lumpishness, its clumsiness, the way it sank into the air, heavy and indigestible. With all the things they couldn't help, surely this one they could have avoided.

"Don't be surprised," I said, "if some day I get it changed legally."

"Gittel by you would have been any better?"

"That was your mother's hard luck, so why does it have to be mine?"

"A dead woman, she never met, she feels free to insult—God knows what she'll say about me after I'm gone!"

"Be reasonable, Ma. Why should I be punished just because *your* mother got stuck with that name?"

"Well, what's good enough for you then?" my sister broke in.

"Gladys? Gloria?"

(Gretchen—Guinevere—Giselle. . . . Goldilocks, you'll never be.)

"If you ask me, " Bernice went on, "she's just cheap. She's really a very cheap person. She puts on an air of being educated, but deep down she's just a loud-mouthed, foul-mouthed brat—"

"*Kinder, kinder!*" My mother predictably threw up her hands, while I marked the scene down as pure James T. Farrell, and went on with what I was doing.

What kept me going at the time was my belief that the life I saw unfolding around me was really a form of literature. Hurrying through the monumental financial district on pea-soup mornings I was back in the City of London, where Carl Sandburg fog crept in on little cat feet. The badly-ventilated hall we occupied at Consolidated Utilities was The Enormous Room, and thinking of Sue-Ellen's lost advantages, I recited Auden to myself:

> But joy is mine not yours—to have come so far,
> Whose cleverest invention was lately fur;
> Lizards my best once who took years to breed,
> Could not control the temperature of blood.

Sue-Ellen herself, an amalgam of Edith Wharton and Sinclair Lewis, was a puzzling instance. I couldn't comprehend how such relative refinement of background—the private French and music lessons, the riding habits and real pearls, the home leather-bound library—could accompany such paper-doll-cut-out flatness of belief. She really had it in for any person who didn't seem to be pulling his weight:

"I saw an item in *The Trib* the other day," she'd say, "about this porter who was earning perfectly decent wages, and at the same time his wife was collecting *sixty dollars* a month on Home Relief!" She'd look straight at me, as though I'd been in on the swindle. "There's your Mr. Roosevelt for you," she'd say; though except for purposes of rebuttal I was no great admirer of the man myself. Instead of too much, I felt he was doing too little.

"Boondogglers and deadbeats," she'd sum up, her pale eyes examining the messy record in front of her, which from upside down I could see was sprinkled with a disgraceful number of

"XX's" "***'s," "OO's," and "+++++'s."

"Impossible social conditions"—I'd toss the ball back to where she wanted it. "The widening gap between the rich and the poor. The need for more drastic solutions . . ."

"Did you know" (she put it to me straight, one day) "that Lenin's name was really V. I. Ulanov, and Stalin's was Dzhugashvili?" Apparently she'd got it from the Red Network that they'd been using false passports, all these years.

"That's nothing," I said, with a feeling of pride that rapidly passed into a sensation of self-betrayal, "Leon Trotsky was born Lev Davidovich Bronstein."

"Is that so?" She took out a pencil and wrote it down in a little notebook. I don't know how far, to what high circles, that piece of information got disseminated.

I'm afraid there were bad days when Sue Ellen, The Red Network, the toilet bells and *The Trib* got mixed up into a common threat, when I saw the eyes of the Brink's guards flicker as I passed their armored trucks, thought I heard clipped instructions pass from mouth to mouth, felt the hands reach slowly for the holster, behind my back.

On better days, when I reflected that there were only four weeks left to go and that everyone seemed to be getting worn down and blasé about all those evidences of fiscal irresponsibility—that likely we'd get to the end of the alphabet without hearing my family held up to public dishonor—I could relax, and find Sue-Ellen's tartness amusing. Unfortunately, we had more than last names in common, because she was the only other person at our table who read books. She read constantly, and fairly selectively, and more than I. She'd gone through Proust twice, in the original, while I was ashamed to admit that I'd got lost in Scott-Moncrieff, within a budding grove.

But my goodness, we couldn't even agree on these high grounds. She'd given up on Thomas Mann because he'd turned out to be a Red; John Steinbeck was a fine stylist, but an unprincipled bleeding heart. For myself, not having the perseverance to finish Proust, I renounced him as decadent. Out of the sides of our mouths—under the eyes of the strolling inspectors—we tossed these high opinions backward and forward while the other two did their best to concentrate on the job at hand.

Of the four at the table, Sue-Ellen was the oldest, by five years or more. Fern Kahn, just out of college like myself, was two years younger than I. Such precociousness! Such perfect orthodontia! It was obvious she too came from Good Family, though being Jewish and solidly middle class, not as good as Sue-Ellen, in fact nowhere as good. But good enough for her and Sue-Ellen to share a certain calm understanding when I began raging off, as I did sometimes, about the bosses and inhuman working conditions and the need for sweeping upheavals. . . . I think that Fern, perfect smile and all, may have been a little frightened of me, something I wasn't able to recognize because all I had to deliver, I knew, were verbal bullets. Any 120-pound weaking could have double twisted my arms behind my back. It never occurred to me that I packed my own ammunition . . . There was also Corrine, a lumpish and unmemorable person, who claimed to be a graduate nurse, though more likely nurse's aide, or ward attendant.

Fern, Corrine, and I would sit down between bells in the company cafeteria, but Sue-Ellen had some peculiar habits. For one, she never ate lunch. Occasionally she'd take out a hunk of a heel of bread, to gnaw on during the lunch break, simply as a matter of dental prophylaxis, because for someone so young, her teeth were already coming loose in her head. She never bought a book, preferring to get them out of the public library, as the need arose. Then, she'd occasionally appear in some preposterous outfit, clearly designed before the Great Crash, which made her look as though she'd stepped out of a silent-era film. "Feel the fabric," she'd say, when we set eyes on the dropped waistline, the hem that tickled the knees. "Feel it," She-Ellen urged. "You'll never get your hands on anything as good in your lifetime. It's a Paris copy of a Patou. My mother picked it up on her last trip over on the *Île de France*."

By then I'd found out that she and the widowed mother occupied a wonderful apartment in a not so wonderful neighborhood, and the extra space which had been standing idle had been let out to roomers; which far from being a disaster, had brought some perfectly lovely people into their lives.

* * *

What strengthened me in my personal decision was the thought that our place was too small with me around, anyway. But I wasn't going to say a word about it until the end.

"How much longer, Goldie?" my mother would ask every Friday, as I handed over my pay. "Three weeks? Two weeks?"

"It's hard to say," I hedged. "New working conditions. A change of schedule . . ."

Bernice was getting restless.

"It's ridiculous—look what she's bringing in, and it's not going to last forever either, when I could be earning almost double—. I called Allied last week, and heard there's a good chance of getting my old job back. If *she*, or someone, would help out for a while. . . ." My mother shook her head. Little short of death, I knew, would have allowed her to step into Bernice's shoes, because that would have meant accepting the breakup as final.

Even with what I was bringing in, there'd been recent trouble, including one near catastrophe at the store: because you could always make a picnic out of eating cold cuts, at home, in the candlelight, but what customer was going to appreciate the convenience of making her selections in the dark?

My father seemed to be growing unhealthily inactive these past weeks. His prickly jaws had a sunk-in look where the back teeth ought to be. Maybe I was first beginning to notice. His breath struggled up out of his chest, tired, tired; he complained of headaches, heartburn, rheumatism, and palpitations. He flopped into the nearest chair like a man who hadn't described the agony of sitting around all day with nothing but time on your hands. There were days when no customer walked in, though they'd put a dressmaker's dummy draped with satin and a bright lamp in the window to make a display. I was growing nervous about my plans, and if there'd been one person around to confide in, I would have talked myself out of the whole adventure.

When I got my mother and sister together, I tried to break it to them gently. "You know, someday I might find myself living in New York."

"What do you want to do *there*?"

"Uh, work in publishing. Be a writer."

"Don't worry," Bernice said, "you'll get married. Why don't

you fix up your hair?"

At work, edginess was in the air. With a promised fifty-dollar bonus as carrot-stick for getting the job finished on time, a new spirit of disorder crept in among us. Loud quarrels erupted, which could be heard halfway down the hall. One table became notorious for the shrieks of laughter that repeatedly seized its occupants. From another, one day, came an uncontrollable fit of crying.

Sue-Ellen was turning sour. At the beginning I hardly noticed, because I'd grown preoccupied with fractions and percentages. I would have liked better security against the Mordecai Wagner case record turning up, against what odds I wasn't prepared to estimate, here, at our table. Even if Corrine or Fern passed it by in contemptuous or charitable silence, it still would not escape Sue-Ellen, who reviewed every piece we touched. We were finishing up the *R*'s, now, heading into the *S*'s, and I wasn't going to breathe easy until we got to *X*. But if I walked out before the end, I would forfeit that fifty-dollar bonus, which nobody in my family knew about or was counting on.

I was picturing to myself the day I boarded a Greyhound headed East, one-way ticket in hand, when Sue-Ellen snapped me up out of dreaming. "Wake up!" she said. "If you're going to sleep, you may as well stay in bed where you can stretch out and feel comfortable."

As I shook my head and tried to look alive, she murmured a rebuke about people who didn't believe in work in the first place, and lacked team spirit.

Well, I thought, she had a point; those fifty dollars meant something to her too—otherwise, why was she here?—and if my dozing endangered our finishing on schedule, justice was on her side. After that, I tried to keep awake and cut down on unneccesary socializing.

But Sue-Ellen couldn't seem to leave me be.

"Aren't you bored with pinko writers?" she asked one morning, as I plunked a Modern Library *Man's Fate* down with my bag and gloves. What I chose to read during my ride to work hardly came under her dispensation. "How much of your pay is going into Party dues?" she asked sarcastically. "When are the Comrades going to march on Washington?"—Grossly unfair wit, because I'd already confided in an unguarded hour how I'd come to realize that political movements were not for me.

Every day a new thing. Nobody there could please her. Her grouchiness extended to Corrine—who, after all this time, couldn't quite seem to master the codes—and to Fern, who virtuously sent down for milk or tomato juice, when the others ordered black coffee.

"Aren't you healthy enough?" Sue-Ellen asked her. "Didn't your mother feed you enough cod-liver oil?"

She was becoming an incredible pill, and I began to revise my estimate on how reading maketh a full human being. When Sue-Ellen appeared among us of a morning her pale eyes were swollen, red rimmed. She kept rubbing them all day long—I forced myself to push down the Jewish mother, who urged her to stop. Maybe her teeth really were coming loose in her head. They seemed unduly visible all of a sudden, thrusting forward her short upper lip. The cropped, delicate nose and narrow jaws which I chose to interpret as patrician bones seemed to have grown more prominent, while her cheeks had fallen in, and gone hollow. And instead of a careless elegance, she was sinking into a frousty and faded dowdiness. Some of the outfits she appeared in looked as though they'd been pulled, in a half-sleep, out of the back of a dark closet—rather than Paris copies, discards left behind by one of the roomers.

At home, they begin telling me how bad I was getting to look.

"Is there such an emergency, you have to work overtime every day?"

"I told you, Ma, we're in a big rush, we promised we'd stay and see this thing through."

I wasn't eating so well at night either . . . Bernice's cooking was finally driving me out, I decided, same as Marvin. And with insufficient rest or nourishment inside me, I was taking on unnecessary tasks—

"Do you suddenly have to wash and iron everything you own? Why are you bringing all your good things down to the cleaners? You'll have time for all this mending and sewing after your job is over—why ruin your eyes at night?"

"Maybe," Bernice suggested, "she's putting together a trousseau."

"What's wrong, Golda?"

My mother walked into my room, where I stood contemplating

stacks of books, my collected journals from the age of thirteen, a scrapbook of high-school and college publications, and two cardboard gift boxes filled with manuscripts. I had to be prepared for a quick getaway. If I didn't walk out first thing on the morning of March 16, I knew I'd never work up the resource to do it again.

"Who said anything's wrong?"

All the chicken fat rendered in a lifetime had manufactured wrinkles in her throat, had sunk crow's-feet deep around her eyes. She was a short lady, and would never aspire to a taller being. She competently balanced my childhood between her small hands like a plucked chicken—one false move and I'd land weeping back in her arms, a case of solidified regret. It was a heart-dissolving moment; but instead of opening, I felt a little, closed knob inside me tighten.

"I'm pulling myself together," I said softly. "I've got a lot to accomplish. Please, Ma—can I be alone?"

For the next couple of days, I did wonder if I'd go through with it. After all, who was I? Just a neighborhood kid from Kedzie Avenue. We were unassuming people. Nobody from my family before me had gone past high school. All very well, those seven-league strides through Humboldt Park at twilight, possibility lighting up the sky like fireworks; but when I stepped on that bus I was going to need more than a certain flare of promise. Some extra backing was needed—I was going to have to pick up the strength from somewhere.

These last few days, Sue-Ellen had turned quite simply beastly. Fern Kahn stopped talking to her, then made it up out of the sweetness of Fern's nature. Corrine she had so terrorized that the girl came in one morning, rested her head on her arms, and admitted the codes had evaporated overnight from her head. We conducted ourselves daily like people in a munitions plant—fearful of the sudden move that might set off the next explosion.

"And I can't say I think much of your James Juice either. Tell me, what do you see in him?"

"Juice?"

"Jerce Joyce."

Sue-Ellen had a bad headache from sitting up reading, late, the night before.

"The character he shows us in the *Portrait* is bad enough, but what kind of human being is he presenting in this one, anyway? Incapable of loyalty to his background or faith, so out of spite he's throwing everything else out too—"

"If you're having trouble with reading *Ulysses* at the beginning," I said, "you might do better to use a guide, and a copy of the—"

"That school you went to," she said irrelevantly, "they're overly partial to your point of view. I know, it's a real hotbed. I was offered a chance by some people who were interested in my education, but I wouldn't go near the place. Why, Walgreen pulled his own niece out, when he discovered she was being force-fed Marx and Engels. . . ."

Sue-Ellen was actually wild this morning. She paraded her dishevelments the way she paraded the soft limp hair she'd stopped bothering to do anything with, the odd rags that made her stand out in a crowd. Some spool in her had come unwound, and she wasn't troubling anymore to run after it or draw it in.

She paused to wipe her eyes.

"Oh, I suppose," she said, "it makes you real proud—must give you quite a thrill—probably makes you feel ecstatic, to be against everything *our* people stand for."

By now the others were delicately looking the other way. She'd never gone this far before.

"It's not that I'm so much against . . ." I stopped, to see what had suddenly captured her attention.

It was a fascinating record that Sue-Ellen was glaring down at. As an aid to concentration, she blew her nose, then wiped her glasses. Someone had scrawled "OO's," "***'s," "XX's," and "+++++'s" all over it, the way Jehovah had visited plagues on the heartless Egyptians: hardly a clean spot that had not been encoded and overlaid with evidences of failure. I was so engrossed with making out the name and address, upside down, that I barely noticed Sue-Ellen's absorption had shifted to the record lying on top, in front of me.

Silently and avidly, our lips barely moving, upside down we were deciphering the document in the other person's keeping. Hard to make a real choice between them—in any race they would have arrived at the finish neck and neck. They were both of them real winners. Mr. Mordecai Wagner, Mrs. Patricia Wagner, lay exposed to the world but fastidiously facing out, beyond, away from one another. Until, in a perfect comradely movement, Sue-Ellen and I reached across the table, and exchanged histories.

CONTRIBUTORS

CHERYL ANN ALEXANDER was born in Trinidad and grew up in Harlem. She is a black, West Indian, radical lesbian feminist, ex-biologist who is just beginning to be published (in addition to "Exile" she has a story forthcoming in *Common Lives, Lesbian Lives*) and is very excited about finally starting her real life at age forty.

ROBIN BECKER lives and works in Cambridge, Massachusetts, where she teaches in the Writing Program at M.I.T. A collection of her poems, *Backtalk,* was published by Alice James Press in 1982. She is co-poetry editor of *Bay Windows,* a Boston newspaper, and serves on the editorial board for *The Women's Review of Books.*

BECKY BIRTHA is a black lesbian feminist who writes poetry and book reviews as well as short stories. She is the author of *For Nights Like This One: Stories of Loving Women* (Frog in the Well, 1983). Born in Hampton, Virginia, in 1948, she currently lives in downtown Philadelphia with her companion of the past eight years. Their relationship is an interracial one.

RUTH GELLER is the author of three books: *Seed of a Woman* (Imp Press, 1979), a novel about the re-emergence of the women's move-ment in the late sixties; *Pictures from the Past* (Imp Press, 1980), a short story collection that includes the story in this anthology; and *Triangles* (Crossing Press, 1984), a novel about a woman trying to make sense of her place in the world. Her fiction and essays have been published in a variety of publications, as well as in the anthol-ogy *Nice Jewish Girls* (Crossing Press).

LINDA HOGAN (Chickasaw) is the author of *Calling Myself Home, Eclipse* (UCLA Indian Studies Center Press), *Seeing Through the Sun* (University of Massachusetts Press) and *That Horse,* a group of stories from Pueblo of Acoma Press. She has recently moved to

Minnesota from Idledale, Colorado, and is teaching at the University of Minnesota in Minneapolis

WILMA ELIZABETH MCDANIEL was born in 1918 in the section of Oklahoma known as the Creek Nation of the Creek Indians. She has a small amount of Cherokee blood. She was raised to middle teens in that rural area and then made the Dustbowl-Great Depression Exodus to California, where she still lives in a house with a wide crack from the many earthquakes in the San Joaquin Valley. Her work has been published in *Broomstick*.

VALERIE MINER's new novel, *Winter's Edge*, about two old women in San Francisco's Tenderloin, will be published in fall, 1985 by the Crossing Press. Her other novels are *Blood Sisters, Movement* and *Murder in the English Department*. She is co-author of *Her Own Woman* (essays) and *Tales I Tell My Mother* (short stories). She has written about women in Africa, Latin America, Asia, Europe and North America. Her work reflects cross-class and cross-cultural movement among women. She is a first generation American who grew up in a working class Scottish-Irish family.

JANICE MIRIKITANI, third-generation Japanese American, is a poet, choreographer, teacher and community organizer. She is Program Director of Glide Church/Urban Center, a multiracial and multicultural institution in San Francisco. Her poetry and short fiction have been anthologized and published in numerous magazines and textbooks, as well as collected in her book, *Awake in the River* (Isthmus Press, San Francisco). She has edited *Aion* magazine, *Third World Women, Time to Greez! Incantations from the Third World*, and most recently, *Ayumi, A Japanese American Anthology*.

BARBARANEELY has previously been published in *Essence* and *Southern Exposure* magazines, as well as in two anthologies, *Speaking for Ourselves* and *Test Tube Women*. She is currently working on a sociopolitical fantasy novel.

PAMELA PAINTER is a founding editor of *StoryQuarterly*, a literary magazine for the short story and has taught fiction workshops in the Harvard Extension Program since 1980. Her collection of short stories, *Getting to Know the Weather,* is forthcoming from the University of Illinois Press in 1985.

TARA REED has been writing since she was twelve. She has read her work at women's gatherings across the country. She now lives in Seattle, where she practices hypnotherapy, massage and the piano.

SARAH SCHULMAN is a the author of *The Sophie Horowitz Story,* a lesbian detective novel from Naiad Press. She is co-author, with Robin Epstein, of two plays, *Art Failures* and *Whining and Dining.* In collaboration with Susan Young, she has developed two performances, *The Swashbuckler* (based on the story by Lee Lynch) and *When We Were Very Young: Radical Jewish Women on the Lower Eastside 1879–1919* (based on Sarah's original research). She is currently finishing a new novel, *Girls, Visions and Everything,* about Jack Kerouac, Blanche Du Bois and assorted lesbians in Reagan's American.

VICKIE L. SEARS is a Cherokee/Spanish/English woman who lives in Seattle; she is a writer, teacher and feminist therapist. Her poetry and fiction have appeared in *Sinister Wisdom, Calyx, Backbone, Ikon,* and *Gathering Ground: New Writing and Art by Northwest Women of Color* (The Seal Press, 1984).

EVELYN SHEFNER has published short stories in *O. Henry Prize Stories 1969, Southern Review, Colorado Quarterly, Eureka Review, Mississippi Review, Negative Capability* and other literary quarterlies. She has held writing fellowships at Yaddo and the MacDowell Colony, and was awarded a creative writing fellowship by the National Endowment for the Arts, 1979.

CELIA SMITH moved from Chicago to Seattle six years ago. Her stories have appeared in *Perihelion*, *Shrew* and *The Northwest Passage*.

ELAINE STARKMAN is co-editor of *State of Peace: The Women Speak*, an anthology of women's peace poems (Gull Press, 1985), and author of a play on Beate Klarsfeld, the German-born Nazi hunter. Her works appear in *The Woman Who Lost Her Names*; *Ariadne's Thread: A Collection of Contemporary Women's Journals*; and *Between Ourselves: Letters Between Mothers & Daughters, 1750–1982*. Presently she is on the editorial board of *Lilith* and teaches at Diablo Valley College in northern California.

EDITORS

FAITH CONLON grew up in New Jersey. She has worked in publishing for several years and joined the Seal Press collective in 1982. She is currently involved in organizing around economic issues and is a founder of the Women's Economic Rights Coalition. Her secret ambition is to postpone all meetings until next year.

RACHEL DA SILVA is a founding member of Seal Press. Her previous editorial experience includes the first four books in Seal's *Backbone* series (1977–1982) and *We Are Ordinary Women* (1985). When not printing books or telemark racing she practices her constructive criticism.

BARBARA WILSON was born and raised in Long Beach, California. She is the author of three collections of stories and two novels, most recently *Murder in the Collective* (Seal Press, 1984). Her translation of the stories of Norwegian author Cora Sandel will appear fall, 1985. She is often the subject of constructive criticism.

ADVISORY BOARD

BETH BRANT is 44, a Bay of Quinte Mohawk and a Taurus. She is editor of *A Gathering of Spirit, Writing and Art by North American Indian Women* (Sinister Wisdom Books, 1983) and the author of *Mohawk Trail,* a collection of poetry and prose (Firebrand Books, 1985). She lives in Detroit, Michigan.

JACQUELINE DE ANGELIS was born and raised in Youngstown, Ohio, and has lived in Los Angeles for the past fifteen years. Her first book of fiction, *The Main Gate,* was published in 1984 by Paradise Press. Along with Aleida Rodríguez she is co-founder and editor of *rara avis* magazine and Books of a Feather press. She received a writer-in-residence fellowship from Dorland Mountain Colony in 1984.

RUTH GELLER: "I have been writing, and teaching writing, for over fourteen years, am the author of three books and numerous articles and stories, and have a Ph.D. in English. I am an Ashkenazi Jew of a mixed class background marriage, and was raised during the repressive McCarthy era of the 1950s. I am forty years old, have been happily married to a wonderful woman for over thirteen years, and have recently decided that I am getting more handsome with age. I dislike defining myself not because of what definitions identify, but because of what they leave out."

KAZU IIJIMA: "I was born in 1918, just after World War I (Kazu is the Japanese character for peace) in Oakland, California, where I attended public schools and graduated from the University of California. I got politicized in college but sisters and I were herded into internment camps along with 110,000 other people of Japanese ancestry during World War II. I was married while in camp (Topaz, Utah) to a soldier already in the Army, assigned to the 442nd Combat Team (all Japanese-American regiment), and I was allowed to leave camp to join him in Hattiesberg, Mississippi (traumatic experience) where he was training. When he was sent overseas, I joined my sister in New York. On his return, we had two children and I am now a grandmother of two. I've been involved in political work since coming to New York—a woman friend and I helped to organize the Asian movement here. I've had editorial jobs, been involved in short story and playwriting workshops, and have done a lot of political writing (newsletters, journals, etc.). I am now a retiree from bread-and-butter work but not from political activity, with special focus on the women's movement as a member of the Organization of Asian Women."

ALEIDA RODRÍGUEZ was born in the village of Güines, Cuba six years before the Revolution. For the past eighteen years she has lived in Los Angeles where she writes and is co-publisher, along with Jacqueline De Angelis, of Books of a Feather. She was a recipient of NEA Creative Writing Fellowship in Poetry.

MARJ SCHNEIDER: "I was born in Minneapolis in 1958 in the sign of Libra. For the past ten years I have worked in various ways to change conditions for blind people and women. In 1980 I found my calling in life with the creation of the Womyn's Braille Press."

EVELYN C. WHITE is a journalist who writes about a variety of black, feminist and cultural issues. Her book, *Chain Chain Change: For Black Women Dealing with Physical and Emotional Abuse*, will be published by The Seal Press in fall, 1985. She holds degrees from the Columbia University Graduate School of Journalism and Wellesley College.